Theories of Development and Underdevelopment

Also of Interest

†*The Gap Between Rich and Poor: Contending Perspectives on the Political Economy of Development,* edited by Mitchell A. Seligson

†*Theories of Comparative Politics: The Search for a Paradigm,* Ronald H. Chilcote

†*Dependency and Marxism: Toward a Resolution of the Debate,* edited by Ronald H. Chilcote

†*From Dependency to Development: Strategies to Overcome Underdevelopment and Inequality,* edited by Heraldo Muñoz

†*Issues in Third World Development,* edited by Kenneth C. Nobe and Rajan K. Sampath

†*Women in Third World Development,* Sue Ellen M. Charlton

†*International Political Economy Yearbook,* edited by W. Ladd Hollist and F. LaMond Tullis

Bibliography on Economic Cooperation Among Developing Countries, 1981–1982, with Annotations, The Research Centre for Cooperation with Developing Countries, Ljubljana, Yugoslavia

Private Voluntary Organizations as Agents of Development, edited by Robert F. Gorman

Development and Crisis in Brazil, 1930–1983, Luiz Bresser Pereira

The State and Underdevelopment in Spanish America: The Political Roots of Dependency in Peru and Argentina, Douglas Friedman

†*The Third World Coalition in International Politics,* Robert A. Mortimer

Comparative Development Perspectives, edited by Gustav Ranis, Robert L. West, Cynthia Taft Morris, and Mark Leiserson

Undermining Rural Development with Cheap Credit, edited by Dale W Adams and Douglas H. Graham

Implementing Rural Development Projects: Nine Critical Problems, edited by Elliott R. Morss and David D. Gow

International Dimensions of Land Reform, edited by John D. Montgomery

Unfinished Agenda: The Dynamics of Modernization in Developing Nations, Manning Nash

†Available in hardcover and paperback.

About the Book and Author

Theories of Development and Underdevelopment
Ronald H. Chilcote

Professor Chilcote offers a critical assessment and clarification of the diverse and often obscure literature and ideas on development and underdevelopment. Examining the origins and evolution of major theories, he first considers the importance of classical writers, especially Marx, Lenin, and Trotsky, then emphasizes views formulated after the Second World War, distinguishing between views of nationalist development, internal colonialism, and dependent capitalist development, on the one hand, and those of the new dependency, subimperialism, and imperialism, on the other. Attention is given to such important thinkers as Osvaldo Sunkel, Celso Furtado, González Casanova, Fernando Henrique Cardoso, Silvio Frondizi, Sergio Bagú, Caio Prado Júnior, Theotonio dos Santos, Ruy Mauro Marini, Aníbal Quijano, Luis Vitale, Ernest Mandel, Paul Baran, André Gunder Frank, Walter Rodney, Immanuel Wallerstein, Samir Amin, and Arghiri Emmanuel.

In the final section of the book, new directions in development theory are identified, including theories of modes of production and the internationalization of capital. Professor Chilcote also provides a useful glossary of terms in the literature and a full bibliography of major contributions to theories of development and underdevelopment.

Ronald H. Chilcote is professor of political science at the University of California, Riverside. He is founder and managing editor of *Latin American Perspectives* and author and editor of numerous books and articles, including *Latin America: The Struggle with Dependency and Beyond; Theories of Comparative Politics: The Search for a Paradigm* (Westview, 1981); and *Dependency and Marxism: Toward a Resolution of the Debate* (Westview, 1982).

Theories of
Development and
Underdevelopment

Ronald H. Chilcote

Westview Press / Boulder and London

Copyright © 1984 by Westview Press, Inc.

Published in 1984 in the United States of America by Westview Press, 5500 Central Avenue, Boulder, Colorado 80301; Frederick A. Praeger, Publisher

Library of Congress Cataloging in Publication Data
Chilcote, Ronald H.
    Theories of development and underdevelopment.
    Bibliography: p.
    1. Economic development.   2. Developing countries.
3. Dependency.   4. Imperialism.   I. Title.
HD82.C513 1984   338.9   84-11875
ISBN 0-8133-0036-3
ISBN 0-8133-0037-1 (pbk.)

Printed and bound in the United States of America

10   9   8   7   6   5   4   3   2   1

Contents

Preface

This book has evolved through a process of interaction with students and colleagues. A variety of courses and classroom experiences stimulated me to write several journal articles on questions of underdevelopment and dependency, and I also benefited from the intense debates over the notion of dependency in the journal *Latin American Perspectives*. Interaction with my fellow editors of this journal and with undergraduate and graduate students helped me to become familiar with the various positions, to distinguish between reformist and revolutionary lines of thinking, to comprehend Marxist as well as non-Marxist theory, and to find my way through the amorphous literature. These experiences made it possible for me to move forward quickly into a penetrating look at the field. I decided to prepare a series of formal lectures for presentation in undergraduate courses. Rough drafts of notes, based on some ten to fifteen hours of research and writing, were prepared for each of seventeen topics. After each lecture, these notes were revised and immediately typed on a word processor, and a copy was placed on reserve in my university library. Students were asked to write comments on them and prepare for discussion and review. With this input I turned to further revision and preparation of a draft that consolidated the seventeen topics into six chapters. In this process I presented the material to nine students in my graduate course on comparative politics. These students divided into three groups and devoted six weeks to reviewing and critically assessing my manuscript. Their feedback, suggestions, and criticisms were taken into account in a third draft. After receiving comments from several colleagues, a final draft was prepared for publication.

This book is the product of an exhausting, yet exhilarating, experience. It is especially gratifying to have been able to combine research and writing with classroom teaching and learning and to end a long process of debate and interaction with the publication of material that should be useful to both scholars and students.

It would be impossible to identify and acknowledge all the persons associated with this work, but I must mention some of them. In particular, I am grateful for the involvement of a number of graduate students: Lisa Durán, Dwight Hahn, Stylianos Hadjiyannis, Dariush Haghighat, Mal Hyman, Ibrahim Osman, Claudia Pompan, Gerry Riposa,

Vicki Fedor-Thurman, Mohamed Wader, Jim Watson, and Russell White. Their contributions were substantial. I also benefited from the reading and suggestions of Professor James Dietz of California State University, Fullerton, and Barbara Metzger of Laguna Beach. The copyediting of Megan L. Schoeck of Westview Press was especially helpful. I received some support from the Department of Political Science, University of California, Riverside, thanks to Donna Cooney, who facilitated typing assistance and use of a word processor. Cheryl Mendonsa typed part of the first draft and made it available for student use in the library. Susan Gregory typed the remainder of the manuscript and with Debbe Webster incorporated the later revisions. Their help was invaluable. Two small grants from my campus provided funds for some of the typing.

Ronald H. Chilcote

Introduction

This work confronts a dilemma on two levels. On the one hand, scholars and teachers are faced with a massive amount of literature on development and underdevelopment. Generally, the literature makes no attempt to take us back to original ideas and conceptions or to identify the politics and particular positions of the major writers on the subject. The result is widespread confusion and a tendency to reject or accept ideas somewhat indiscriminately. This book attempts to solve this problem. On the other hand, given that the literature is diverse and often obscure, students often find the task of making sense of development and underdevelopment overwhelming. Thus, this book is for students as well as for scholars and teachers.

For nearly two decades I have been teaching two courses, one on politics and development, the other on politics and underdevelopment. Originally, a single course followed in the path of Gabriel Almond and James S. Coleman's pioneering *Politics of Developing Areas* (1960). After the Second World War, the attention of comparativists turned from the advanced world of Europe and the United States to backward and presumably developing areas. It was immediately clear that not very much was known about these areas, for they had been little studied.

The social scientists who met with Almond and Coleman determined that a structural-functional approach focusing not only on institutions and processes of government but also on political parties, interest groups, and other less-defined entities and forces would allow for identification of gaps in knowledge and stimulate new investigation. Students found that approach very unsatisfactory, for it attempted to structure categories of knowledge about such various areas of the Third World as Africa, Asia, and Latin America.

The students' negative reaction resulted in a shift in the content of my course. I turned to the political manifestations and theories of Third World leaders, usually revolutionaries but sometimes reformist politicians willing to work for a moderate change of their political systems. In Africa, Asia, and Latin America, there were demands for change. Kwame Nkrumah and Fidel Castro, for example, were revolutionary leaders who inspired their own people to seek change, and their thought appealed to my students.

Eventually it became clear that, along with the practical experience of the Third World, the various theories of development and underdevelopment had to be examined and understood. During the late sixties and early seventies, I introduced my students to theories of dependency and underdevelopment and to case studies of various situations in Africa and Latin America. I also made use of some innovative techniques designed to stimulate learning and involvement in the classroom; in particular, students critically examined opposing perspectives of development, then they were encouraged to formulate a personal position on essential issues and to build support for their stance (Chilcote, Gorman, LeRoy, and Sheehan 1975).

More recently, I began to encourage them to take a closer look at these theories. First, I considered it essential for them to identify and study the ideas of the classical writers, especially Marx, who wrote about the devastating impact of British capital on India and Ireland, but also Lenin, who emphasized capitalist development in Russia and monopoly capitalism as the highest stage of imperialism, and Trotsky, who called for permanent revolution among backward and advanced nations throughout the world and advocated a theory of uneven and combined development.

Second, I wanted students to examine the origins of contemporary thinking. In particular, this examination necessitated a review of writers whose ideas on underdevelopment first became known after the Second World War. Most critical assessments of the literature have taken us back to Raúl Prebisch, who formulated the early division of the world into center and periphery and sought solutions to the negative consequences of capitalist penetration in Latin America. Prebisch and the Economic Commission for Latin America advocated autonomous capitalist development through measures that would stem the impact of outside investment. Celso Furtado and Osvaldo Sunkel followed in this direction, and Pablo González Casanova and Fernando Henrique Cardoso used the center-periphery formulation in their own unique and imaginative views, respectively known as internal colonialism and dependent capitalist development. All these writers were associated with capitalism and the reformist tradition.

Ideas centered around socialism and what I characterize as the revolutionary tradition evolved at about the same time. Silvio Frondizi, Sergio Bagú, and Caio Prado Júnior all offered perspectives on the negative consequences of capitalism. They argued that capitalism had implanted itself in Latin America since the sixteenth century and was responsible for the poverty and exploitation so evident there today. They favored the overthrow of capitalism and the establishment of socialism as the means for overcoming backwardness in their countries.

Their writing provided a basis for ideas such as the new dependency of Theotonio dos Santos, the subimperialism of Ruy Mauro Marini, and the imperialism and dependency of Aníbal Quijano. Many of these ideas were incorporated in the thought of such Trotskyists as Luis Vitale and Ernest Mandel.

The revolutionary thrust also appeared in the writings of Paul Baran and André Gunder Frank, who emphasized trade and markets within the capitalist world to explain how capitalism promotes underdevelopment. Although they referred to capitalism in general terms, they were concerned especially with merchant capital and its influence on Third World economies. Immanuel Wallerstein and Samir Amin related merchant capital to the world system, Wallerstein focusing on the origins and evolution of capitalism in Europe and Amin on capitalism in the periphery.

Third, I wanted to help students compare these various lines of thinking. In this effort, I identified the important ideas of each writer and attempted to describe and explain their implications. This book, then, is a critical review and assessment of the literature on development and underdevelopment. Readers will soon discover the complexity of this literature and, I hope, learn how to make sense of the many political positions and methodologies that permeate it. Eventually, by exploring the original sources cited herein, they should be able to find a personal stance, defend it with facts, and perhaps move on to new and productive areas of inquiry.

1 / The Conceptual Framework

The literature on development and underdevelopment has fascinated scholars and students for more than a generation. The novice must confront thousands of books and journal articles on the subject, representing a myriad of theoretical perspectives and positions. To comprehend this literature, an understanding of certain key concepts is essential. Most explanations of development and underdevelopment refer to the idea of a "third world," a term that is used loosely and variously. It is appropriate, therefore, to begin with a discussion of this term. Other concepts of fundamental importance to our task are capitalism and socialism, state and class, accumulation and reproduction of capital, and development and underdevelopment themselves.

Third World: Myth or Reality?

The plethora of definitions of "third world" suggests that the concept is not very useful theoretically or analytically. One prevailing understanding is linked to the geographical or territorial designation of certain countries in Asia, Africa, and Latin America. Many countries in these areas achieved their independence after the Second World War, and there was a concerted effort, especially on the international diplomatic level, to distinguish them, as newly emerging nations, from those in the capitalist First World and the socialist Second World. This formulation tended to focus on poor people while overlooking the upper strata of poor countries. Thus Venezuela, which has a high per capita income relative to other nations in Latin America, could be described as "emerging" from its backward condition when in fact its poverty is widespread and its wealth is concentrated in a small ruling class whose fortunes are largely a consequence of the petroleum boom. At the same time, Cuba may be considered part of the Third World because of its low per capita income and material standard of living, yet it has no poverty. A geographical designation also tends to overlook poor populations in Hispanic and black America, thereby obscuring Third World social groupings within a First World nation.[1] For this reason, another understanding of "third world," and the one I prefer, emphasizes exploitation and oppression, lack of technology and development, underdevelopment brought about by colonialism and imperialism, and dependency upon the dominant capitalist system and outside influences, wherever in the world these occur.

Leslie Wolf-Phillips has attributed the term "third world" to the French demographer and economic historian Alfred Sauvy, who in 1952, at the height of the Cold War, used it to distinguish developing countries outside the two power blocs. Apparently "third world" and "third force" were used interchangeably in France during the period 1947 to 1949.[2] Peter Worsley has alluded to the use of the term by Claude Bourdet as early as April 1949, but Joseph L. Love disputes this possibility and suggests an origin in the "third position" of Juan Perón in 1949 and the general usage of Third World after the Afro-Asian Conference in Bandung in 1955.[3] In the United States, the Committee for the Study of Comparative Politics of the Social Science Research Council began to study the political institutions and processes of the Third World in the late fifties.[4]

Several refinements of the term have been set forth by Third World leaders. African leaders such as Kwame Nkrumah have used Third World in the sense of political nonalignment of a bloc of nations that would stand apart from and help to reconcile the Cold War differences between East and West. Nkrumah mentioned Frantz Fanon, who wrote in *The Wretched of the Earth* (1963) that the people of the Third World saw capitalist exploitation as their enemy and were committed to a noncapitalist road. Nkrumah argued that this path did not imply passivity and an escape from the struggle between the two worlds of capitalism and socialism:

> The world struggle, and the cause of world tension, has to be seen not in the old political context of the cold war, that is, of nation states and power blocs, but in terms of revolutionary and counter-revolutionary peoples. It cuts right across territorial boundaries and has nothing to do with colour or race. It is a war to the finish between the oppressed and the oppressors, between those who pursue a capitalist path and those committed to socialist policies. [Nkrumah 1968, 464]

He concluded that there really are only two worlds, one revolutionary and socialist and the other counterrevolutionary and capitalist with its extensions of imperialism and colonialism. Therefore, Third World is a "misused expression which has come to mean everything and nothing." The Third World cannot be separated from the socialist world but is an integral part of it, committed to the struggle against capitalism to end the exploitation of people (Nkrumah 1968, 465).[5]

Mao Zedong revised the theory of three worlds by classifying the United States and the Soviet Union, both capitalist superpowers, as the first; Japan, Europe, and Canada, all secondary imperialist countries, along with the revisionist countries of Eastern Europe as the second; and the rest of Asia and the whole of Africa and Latin America as the third. Mao viewed the relationships among these worlds as conditioned by the imperialism and hegemony of the two superpowers, the first world exploiting and dominating the third while the second world, also attempting to dominate the third, is in turn subject to the first. Thus, according to Mao, power is the basis for this global differentiation, and given that the Soviet Union represents the greatest threat, the third world, the second world, and the United States should form a united front.[6] Albania, once a close ally of China against the Soviet Union, criticized this model for minimizing the contradiction between imperialism and socialism on a world scale and between the bourgeoisie and the proletariat in advanced capitalist countries. Albania also denied that the imperialist countries of the second world could assume a progressive role and that the United States was any less a danger than the Soviet Union.[7]

By the middle seventies, diplomatic circles were referring to four worlds, and the literature was designating a capitalist world, a socialist world, a third world of developing nations, and a fourth world of poor, powerless, oppressed, and dispossessed countries (see Hamalian and Karl 1976). Grant McCall proposed a variation of these designations by suggesting that the fourth world include minorities within countries of the other worlds.[8] Worsley (1980, 20) points out that some writers have defined as many as nine worlds for analytical purposes.

These models may be helpful in sorting out data and suggesting classifications of the nations of the contemporary world. Models, however, are heuristic devices, which means that they have limited potential for the analysis of a complex world.

Capitalism and Socialism: Distinctions and Issues

In primitive classless societies, everyone participated in the decisions affecting life in the community and relations between the community and the outside world. Living conditions were poor in this collective society, and the people struggled to survive in the face of the forces of nature. One of the first divisions of labor occurred in ancient times with the appearance of towns and professional artisans who engaged in the production of commodities that they exchanged freely and more or less equally in the market for products they immediately needed. Another division of labor took place with the introduction of money and the appearance of the usurer or merchant specializing in international commerce. In contrast to the more advanced industrial capitalism, merchant capital was an elementary form of capitalism, and it was characterized by social relations whereby the owners of capital appropriated the absolute surplus value produced by workers. Merchant capital was especially conspicuous in Western Europe during the fourteenth to the sixteenth centuries. Modern capitalism is characterized by a clear separation of producers from their means of production and subsistence, the formation of a class that owns and controls these means of production, the bourgeoisie, and the appearance of a class—the proletariat—that owns only its labor and must sell this to the owners of the means of production in order to survive.[9]

Until the late nineteenth century, capitalism was usually characterized by "free" competition, but about that time technology spawned new industries, and capitalists began to form cartels, trusts, and holding companies. A concentration of finance capital (bank capital that penetrates and dominates industry) resulted in a decline of free competitive capitalism and in the growth of monopolies. Lenin (1967) considered finance capital the latest and most highly developed form of capitalism, and he called this state "imperialism." His theory focused on the rapid concentration of production in the large industrial monopolies and the export of capital from advanced nations to less developed parts of the world. Mandel (1975) classified the imperialist era into a classical phase, from the late nineteenth century to the end of the Second World War, and a late phase. Whereas the monopoly was characteristic of the classical phase, the multinational firm was characteristic of the late one.

Socialism implies collective, rather than private, ownership of the major means of production and appropriation of the social surplus product (the production of workers beyond their requirements for subsistence). In the transition period from capitalism to socialism, remnants of capitalism are evident: labor power continues to be sold for wages, some surplus product is appropriated as individual privileges, and a money economy prevails. The new economy may also be managed by bureaucratic elements uncommitted to the principle of political and economic participation by all the people, and private rather than public interest may be a motivating force. The shift from a capitalist mode of production toward a collective mode is apparent only with the overcoming of these tendencies. The struggle for socialism thus involves the replacing of the capitalist state with the workers' state, the substitution of proletarian democracy for bourgeois democracy. The provision for the basic needs of all the people, usually under a planned economy, becomes a priority. The goals of the socialist society are the creative use of work and leisure and the elimination of a commodity and money economy; inequality, classes, and the state; and alienated labor. The achievement of these goals would lead to communism, a higher stage of socialism.

State and Class

The state evolved as functions performed by all the people in primitive, classless societies were assumed by separate groups of people—for instance, as soldiers, judges, and hereditary rulers took over ordinary citizens' tasks of arming and protecting themselves, judging their equals, and choosing leaders for particular activities. These groups exploited and profited from the work of the people over whom they ruled. Marx and Engels, in *The Communist Manifesto*, implied that the state is the instrument of the ruling classes: The executive of the state "is but a committee for managing the affairs of the whole bourgeoisie" (Marx and Engels 1958, 36). Lenin, in *State and Revolution* (1932), argued that the police and standing army were instruments of state power and that the proletariat had to struggle against the state until it disappeared altogether.

Several variants of these ideas are emphasized in the socialist conception of the capitalist state today. The instrumentalist perspective, found in the writing of the English political scientist Ralph Miliband (for example, 1969), stresses that the state is the instrument of and is manipulated by the ruling classes. The structuralist view of Marxists such as Nicos Poulantzas (1973) emphasizes that the state unifies the interests of the bourgeoisie through such structures or apparatuses as the army, police, and judiciary. In contrast to these socialist views, the prevailing understanding of the state in the mainstream literature of political and social science sees it as a political marketplace through which demands and interests of competing individuals and groups filter. Neutral state agencies mediate and mitigate the conflict that emanates from this arena. The state agencies function as bases of political power and struggle for funding support.[10]

Marx believed that all history was the struggle of classes. Under capitalism, he argued, society would eventually polarize into two principal classes, the bourgeoisie and the proletariat. The bourgeoisie had emerged from the merchant class in towns established during the feudal Middle Ages. Then manufacturing replaced production by closed guilds, and a manufacturing class supplanted the guild masters. Modern industry soon took the place of this early manufacturing, along with the invention of machinery, the expansion of markets, and the emergence of a new bourgeoisie with control over the economy and the state. As the ruling class, this bourgeoisie owned the means of production and also ruled politically. In Marx's view, the state under capitalism maintains the property relations of the wealthy minority and thus supports the oppression of one class by another. The state does not stand above classes but always rests on the side of the rulers. Thus, ultimately, this state and the ruling class should be abolished.[11]

Max Weber, in contrast, believed that capitalism is essential to the modern world and argued that the state can legitimately use physical force to ensure harmony and order among diverse interests. He understood politics as "striving to share power or striving to influence the distribution of power, either among states or among groups within a state" (Weber 1958, 78). In other words, the dominance of the state ensures the sanctioning of a plurality of interests. In capitalism, through the rational distribution of organizational tasks within the bureaucracy, the state promotes routinization and efficiency. This perception of the state allowed Weber to view class in purely economic terms. For him, a class exists "when (1) a number of people have in common a specific causal component of their life chances, in so far as (2) this component is represented exclusively by economic interests in the possession of goods and opportunities for income, and (3) is represented under the conditions of the commodity or labor markets" (Weber 1958, 181). He saw each class as comprising many status groups, ranked in accordance with relative market advantage. As market demands change, status groups might be rearranged so as to elevate one and lower another. With this understanding of class, Weber could argue that there exists a great variety of class situations and that class consciousness does not necessarily solidify the working class into a revolutionary force.[12]

In summary, one view of class emphasizes inevitable class confrontation and struggle; the other, harmony among diverse interests. One stresses ownership and control of the means of production as an explanation of the domination and exploitation of one class by another, whereas the other sees various status groups competing for power. One sees the state on the side of the ruling class while the other understands it as a mediating and moderating force that ensures stability and order among all classes and groups. My own position, and one that is increasingly becoming acceptable to contemporary social scientists, is that the ruling class is a dominant bourgeoisie in possession of the major means of economic production and political power. This class need not be simply monolithic but may comprise varied interests that tend to become cohesive. A ruling class is an economic class that rules politically. Usually its monopolization of power is directly related to capitalism and the ownership of the means of production, and it dominates the economy through control over corporations and financial institutions. The ruling class must be considered in relation to the following other classes.[13]

Bourgeoisie. Owners of capital who purchase means of production and labor. They are distinguishable by

1. property relationships, for example, monopolistic bourgeoisie or large owners of industry and banking capital who may have ties with foreign capitalists and imperialism and own factories, insurance companies, banks, and large commercial companies; they may also be large landowners. There is also the *non-monopolistic bourgeoisie*, or owners of certain industrial and commercial firms who are sometimes allied with the monopolistic or foreign bourgeoisie; they may be owners of small industrial and commercial enterprise or middle-sized and small farms; and they tend to be nationalist, sometimes opposed to imperialism.

2. type of capital or means of production possessed: for example, the *agrarian bourgeoisie* of modern landowners who run farms with machinery, pay salaries to workers, and make profits; or traditional landowners who operate large estates, live in cities, and invest little in their land. There also is the *mining bourgeoisie*; the *industrial and commercial bourgeoisie*, usually large owners (sometimes allied with monopolistic or foreign bourgeoisie) but also owners of small enterprise; and the *banking bourgeoisie*.

3. amount of capital owned as differentiated in a *large bourgeoisie, medium bourgeoisie,* or *small bourgeoisie.*

Petty Bourgeoisie. Small capitalists who directly or indirectly control their means of production but, unlike large capitalists, do not possess capital. They may desire to acquire capital or feel oppressed by the bourgeoisie. They may reside in

1. urban areas as *owners* or *tenants* of small artisan industries and businesses or as *independent professionals* (attorneys, some physicians and architects, engineers, artists, writers, teachers, or intelligentsia).

2. rural areas as *sharecroppers, tenant farmers,* etc.

New Middle Class or New Petty Bourgeoisie. Some professionals, bureaucrats, and managers who may influence capitalists but, like workers, do not usually own means of production.

Proletariat. Workers who do not own means of production and who sell their labor power for money. They may be *urban* workers in monopolistic and nonmonopolistic industries and white-collar workers in private or public industry, banks, etc.; or *rural* farmhands and sharecroppers who earn wages.

Peasants. Farmers who do not own their land and usually are associated with precapitalist modes of production, for example, *squatters, renters,* and *unpaid family workers.*

Lumpen Proletariat. Unemployed idle persons, etc.

Primitive Accumulation, Accumulation, and Reproduction of Capital

Necessary production involves labor to satisfy people's basic needs. Beyond satisfaction of food, drink, shelter, rest, and security, people can devote themselves to other economic activity, which may result in a division of labor, the appearance of a surplus product, and an ordering of society into classes. In primitive as well as in advanced societies, it is possible for one class to give up its productive labor and turn to leisure at the expense of other classes. The accumulation of surplus production can then be used to obtain material privileges and advantages.

Primitive communal production consists of labor that collectively participates in and owns the means of production. Primitive accumulation is the process whereby the producers (the laborers) are separated from the means of production. According to Marx, "It appears as primitive, because it forms the pre-history stage of capital and of the mode of production corresponding with it" (Marx 1967, 1:714–715). Thus primitive accumulation is a starting point for capitalism.

Accumulation, in its developed rather than in its primitive form, takes place when the capitalist sells his commodities and converts the money from the sale into capital. Marx described this process as involving three steps. First, money is converted into means of production and labor power: Raw materials are purchased, and workers are hired to produce. Second, the means of production and labor power are converted into commodities whose value contains the capital originally invested, say for the raw materials and labor, plus the surplus value, that is, the additional value created in production. Third, these commodities are sold, resulting in money that is converted anew into capital. This process is called the circulation of capital. The capitalist appropriates unpaid labor from the workers in the form of surplus value, though he must share this surplus value—in the form of, for example, profit, interest, or rent—with other capitalists and landowners who may be involved in the production process (Marx 1967, 1:564–565).

Capitalist production must reproduce itself. Marx says: "The conditions of production are also those of reproduction. No society can go on producing, in other words, no society can reproduce, unless it constantly reconverts a part of its products into means of production, or elements of fresh products" (Marx 1967, 1:566). Thus capitalism must replace equipment, raw materials, and other essentials used in the process of production. Production, of course, must be understood in relation to consumption. The worker, for instance, consumes by her or his production the means of production—for example, the raw material that goes into the product. The capitalist also consumes labor power when paying for the labor in the production process. The worker also turns his or her wages into individual consumption, the provision of food and shelter for subsistence. Unlike others before him, Marx did not treat economic activities such as consumption and production in isolation from each other but dealt with them in an interrelated and dialectical way:

> Production is thus at the same time consumption, and consumption production. Each is simultaneously its opposite. . . . Production leads to consumption, for which it provides the material; consumption without production would have no object. But consumption also leads to production by providing for its products the subject for whom they are products. [Marx and Engels 1973, 131]

Failure to understand this relationship and an overemphasis on consumption to the neglect of production are reflected in some contemporary works that stress the importance of exchange on a national or an international level or that rely upon underconsumption as an explanation for imperialist expansion or on the market or trade as a basis for understanding the backwardness of some nations. Likewise, attention to production without recognition of its counterpart may lead to rigid economistic interpretations. These deficiencies will be apparent later in our review of the thought of some writers.

Development and Underdevelopment

Some interpretations of development and underdevelopment that emphasize the positive accomplishments of capitalism tend to be called diffusionist theories of development, whereas those that stress the negative consequences of capitalism tend to be identified as theories of underdevelopment.

Diffusionist theories are of at least three types. One theory associates democracy with political aspects of development in advanced capitalist nations and can be found in early writings such as James Bryce's *Modern Democracies* (1921) and Carl J. Friedrich's *Constitutional Government and Democracy* (1937). These works emphasize the values and practices of Western democracy, particularly constitutional legitimacy, electoral participation, multiparty systems, and competitive politics. These themes are brought together by Seymour Martin Lipset (1959), who outlines the requisites of democracy along lines of political legitimacy and economic development. These premises of democracy are also incorporated in a focus on political democracy (see, for example, Pye 1966, especially Chapter 4). In addition, the crises and sequences of political development in capitalist states are of interest, in particular how the polity develops through increases in differentiation, equality, and capacity and through crises of identity, legitimacy, participation, penetration, and distribution.[14] Generally, it is assumed, these characteristics appear with the evolution and advancement of capitalism.

A second diffusionist theory is associated with nationalism, a European notion that originated with attention to such cultural traditions as symbols of national experience, including the flag, anthem, parades; institutional solidarity, sovereignty of the state or nation; and a creed of loyalty and common feeling or will associated with the consciousness of the nation in the minds of the people. Historians trace nationalism to the French Revolution and to the unity forged in Germany and Italy during the nineteenth century. More recently, nationalism has been seen in the emerging national states in Africa, Asia, and Latin America. Although there are many varieties of nationalism, a basic assumption runs through the literature: Nationalism provides the ideological impetus and motivation for development. Nationalism is usually associated with capitalist development, but it also is found in societies pursuing socialist alternatives.[15]

A third diffusionist theory implies a linear path toward modernization. Essentially this idea is found in nineteenth-century theories of evolution and in the belief that the Western world would civilize other less developed areas by spreading Western values, capital, and technology. More recently, the U.S. economic historian Walt W. Rostow (1960) outlined stages of economic growth in the direction of modernization, and A.F.K. Organski (1965) examined the development of government through four basic stages. Samuel P. Huntington (1968) stressed control and regulation of rapid social and economic changes so as to avoid the political decay that may result from instability, corruption, authoritarianism, and violence. These theories of development can be criticized as ethnocentric, biased in favor of a particular economic path, ideological in their Western assumption of pluralistic politics, and dogmatic in their insistence upon a continuous progression through historical stages.

Underdevelopment theory is represented by various tendencies. Raúl Prebisch and other economists associated with the United Nations Economic Commission for Latin America (ECLA) once argued that capitalist national development could eventually be brought about by import substitution—placing limitations on imports and establishing an industrial base for the assembly or manufacture of corresponding goods within the nation. In this way a new bourgeoisie, commercial and industrial in character, would emerge. Another theory of underdevelopment is the "internal colonialism" model of Mexican political sociologist Pablo González Casanova (1970b). Here the focus is on the dominance of a metropolitan center within the nation over peripheral areas that have remained "marginal" to national development, indeed exploited, backward, and underdeveloped. This notion was elaborated on a world scale by André Gunder Frank, who argued that the relationship between metropolises, or advanced economic centers, and satellites, or peripheral backward nations, had been a reflection of mercantilist and capitalist expansion since the sixteenth century. Underdevelopment, he believed, was not an original state, but a consequence of the negative impact of capitalism (Frank 1966).

Other writers, among them Emmanuel (1972) and Amin (1976b), have looked at questions of unequal exchange, with attention to transfers of value from the periphery to the center. Unequal international specialization is viewed as a result of distortions in export activities, emphasis on light rather than on heavy industries in the periphery, and other considerations. Because of its integration in the world capitalist market, the periphery is unable to challenge the foreign monopolies and, therefore, cannot develop autonomously. Another explanation for underdevelopment is found in the theory of uneven and combined development (e.g., Novack 1966), which suggests that the growth of productive forces may be faster or slower in one or another segment of society (uneven development) and that features of a lower stage may combine with those of a higher stage (combined development).

These ideas are frequently incorporated into various conceptions of dependency, and attention to theories of imperialism is emphasized by many writers seeking explanations of underdevelopment (see Chilcote 1974, 1981a).

All of these theories of underdevelopment suffer from criticism. The view that a progressive national bourgeoisie will resolve underdevelopment is challenged by the failure of this bourgeoisie. Further, according to critics, autonomous capitalist development is impossible in the face of dominant nations, and internal class relations often are ignored by these theories. Finally, no unified theory of underdevelopment exists, and the various and contradictory tendencies are not always relevant to the historical experience of backward nations.

When the interpretations of development and underdevelopment are applied to historical experience, say, in Western Europe and Latin America, the following descriptions of what happened might be suggested. The diffusionist theories of development would posit that capitalism began to evolve from feudalism in the tenth and eleventh centuries. Within a few centuries, merchants had consolidated control over the towns and penetrated the countryside with new markets. This process was particularly evident in England and less conspicuous on the Iberian Peninsula at the time of the conquest of the Americas. Thus remnants of feudalism were transferred from Spain and Portugal to the New World, a feudal aristocracy emerged in Latin America, and the development of full capitalism was impeded, except in large cities where capitalism grew as a result of commercial contact with more-modern nations. The consequence was two societies, one feudal and backward in the rural countryside and the other capitalist and modern in the urban centers. Thus, for diffusionist theorists, capitalism offers a solution to the problem of backwardness and a path to development.

Theories of underdevelopment would offer a contrasting perspective, positing that during the period of the American conquest, Spain, like England before it, was a country in transition from feudalism to capitalism, a nation of uneven development combining feudal institutions with the activities of an emerging merchant class. Thus the discovery, conquest, and colonization of the Americas were undertaken with the capitalist objectives of exploiting precious metals and incorporating the Americas into a new system of capitalist production. The ruling class that emerged in Latin America was not feudal, but bourgeois, and it exploited the raw materials of the countryside, leaving underdevelopment in its wake. Not two societies but one society emerged, and the wealth and development of the cities could be explained by their underdevelopment of the rural areas. Capitalism was responsible for underdevelopment, and thus only socialism offered the possibility of development.

2 / Classical Interpretations of Development and Underdevelopment

In debating the usefulness of the notions of development and under-development for explanations of the role of capitalism in the contemporary world, only a few scholars have attempted to explore how these terms were used by Marx, Lenin, and Trotsky. Other past thinkers might be mentioned, but these three are important for a number of reasons. Their attention to capitalist accumulation and disaccumulation helps in understanding development and underdevelopment. Their ideas are influential in intellectual circles where issues of development and underdevelopment are debated. Often they are cited by critics claiming to be Marxists, yet they are sometimes misunderstood or misquoted, resulting in confusion.

Marx

Until about 1860, Marx took the position that the worldwide expansion of British industrial capital would devastate noncapitalist societies and establish the conditions for the advance of capitalism outside Europe. As early as 1848, Marx and Engels stated in the *Communist Manifesto* that the thrust of capitalism was embedded in the development of the forces of production: "The bourgeoisie, during its rule of scarce one hundred years, has created more massive and more colossal productive forces than have all preceding generations together." Capitalism, they believed, expands while assimilating other societies under its control: The bourgeoisie "must nestle everywhere, settle everywhere, establish connections everywhere."

> The bourgeoisie, by the rapid improvement of all instruments of production, by the immensely facilitated means of communication, draws all, even the most barbarian, nations into civilization. The cheap prices of its commodities are the heavy artillery with which it batters down all Chinese walls, with which it forces the barbarians' intensely obstinate hatred of foreigners to capitulate. [Marx and Engels, quoted in Brewer 1980, 45]

13

In his articles on India, published in 1853 for the *New York Daily Tribune,* Marx wrote about how the rise of industrial capital had shaped the relationship of Great Britain to India: "It was the British intruder who broke up the Indian hand-loom and destroyed the spinning wheel. England began with driving the Indian cottons from the European market" (Marx and Engels 1979, 128). The towns in which fabrics were produced then declined. Whereas previously the drive of British capital had led to the establishment of landed estates in India and the influx of British textiles, now industrial capital was to establish its mark.

> The more the industrial interest became dependent on the Indian market, the more it felt the necessity of creating fresh productive powers in India, after having ruined her native industry. . . . The manufacturers, conscious of their ascendancy in England, ask now for the annihilation of these antagonistic powers in India, for the destruction of the whole ancient fabric of Indian Government, and for the final eclipse of the East India Company. [Marx and Engels 1979, 154–155]

Marx envisaged "a double mission in India: one destructive, the other regenerating—the annihilation of the old Asiatic society, and the laying of the material foundations of Western society in Asia" (Marx 1943, 67). The British, he said, had brought destruction to India

> by breaking up the native communities, by uprooting the native industry, and by levelling all that was great and elevated in the native society. The historic pages of their rule in India report hardly anything beyond that destruction. The work of regeneration hardly transpires through a heap of ruins. Nevertheless it has begun. [Marx 1943, 13]

According to R. P. Dutt, what Marx meant was that capitalism had created the material conditions that would serve as a basis for a capitalist advance; regeneration itself depended either on a victory of the English proletariat over the ruling class or on the successful revolt of the Indian people (Dutt, in Marx 1943, 14).

Kenzo Mohri has pointed to the emphasis of many writers, including Paul Baran and Samir Amin, on Marx's idea that capitalism would destroy noncapitalist societies—establishing itself in outlying areas, exploiting peoples, and extracting surplus on behalf of advanced capitalist countries. These writers focus on the underdevelopment, rather than the development, left in the wake of capitalist penetration into backward areas. Thus they see capitalism in these areas as regressive rather than progressive, as Marx's writings on India suggested. However, it may be that Baran and some other writers overlooked later writing in which Marx appeared to be moving toward a position in which British free trade was seen as transforming the old society into the world market system so that "the resulting transformation of this society would determine a course of development of its economy and a structure of its productive powers completely dependent on England" (Mohri 1979, 40).[16]

Marx's later writing on the Irish question (see Marx and Engels 1972) more closely resembled contemporary writing on capitalist development of underdevelopment: "A new and international division of labor, a division suited to the requirements of its chief centers on modern industry, springs up and converts one part of the globe into a chiefly agricultural field of production, for supplying the other part which remains a chiefly industrial field" (Marx 1967, 1:451).[17] In the case of Ireland, Marx argued that the Irish needed self-government and independence, agrarian revolution, and protective tariffs against England.[18]

In summarizing Marx's writing on India, Anthony Brewer has identified an important distinction that may help to explain differences in contemporary thinking on development and underdevelopment. Although merchant capital exploits and destroys precapitalist social formations in a backward country, it does not transform them. In contrast, industrial capital both destroys and transforms the old into new social formations and, in this process, promotes new divisions of labor.[19] Merchant capital, Marx believed, predominates wherever backward conditions exist. Commerce prevails through precapitalist stages of social formations while in modern society, the reverse is true. Thus British rule in India created misery and backwardness along with preconditions for capitalist development. Brewer believed that Marx was consistent in his analysis of India and Ireland but that these nations existed at different levels of development. He concluded that capitalism does not necessarily assimilate peripheral areas, though it would exploit them if they exist. "Up to the industrial revolution, capitalism's external relations were mediated through merchant capital, and did not necessarily transform other societies drawn into the world market. Once industrial capital had taken charge, capitalist conquest could play a progressive (though brutal) role initiating capitalist industrialisation" (Brewer 1980, 60).

In his attention to exploitation in India and Ireland, Marx focused on the colonial situation and distinguished rich nations from poor ones. He also delineated a relationship between dominant capital and exploitation of precapitalist areas, and some of his ideas resemble the notion prevalent today that capitalism develops underdevelopment in many parts of the world.

Lenin

In *Imperialism: The Highest Stage of Capitalism* Lenin stated, "Not only are there two main groups of countries, those owning countries, and the colonies themselves, but also the diverse forms of dependent countries which, politically, are independent but in fact are enmeshed in the net of financial and diplomatic dependency" (Lenin 1967, 1:742–743). Several writers have commented on Lenin's contributions to a theory of underdevelopment and dependency. The Brazilian social scientist Fernando Henrique Cardoso acknowledged these contributions but argued that recent changes had affected the pattern of relationship between imperialist and dependent nations. "*Dependency, monopoly capitalism,* and *development* are not contradictory terms: there occurs a kind of *dependent capitalist development* in the sectors of the Third World integrated in the new form of monopolistic expansion" (Cardoso 1973a, 11). Carlos Johnson has suggested that Lenin took the dependent nation concept from non-Marxist political economists but was guided by materialist reasoning and theoretical analysis. Johnson argues that Lenin attacked the Russian Narodniks, or popular socialists, for their idealism and for a petty-bourgeois economic analysis that was similar to contemporary writings emphasizing the concern about a diminishing domestic market, the difficulty of realizing surplus value at home, and the desire for foreign markets in order to appropriate surplus value (Carlos Johnson 1981). In contrast to this view, Stephen Clarkson has expressed optimism for the application of Marxist-Leninist concepts in the analysis of underdevelopment (Clarkson 1972), and David Lane has pointed to Lenin's belief that the bourgeois revolution was only a short intermediary stage in the struggle of nations to overthrow capitalism and has suggested that this view is what has justified the pursuit of noncapitalist development in the underdeveloped nations and inspired writers such as Paul Baran and André Gunder Frank to call for political revolution led by the working class (Lane 1974).

Many of the ideas about the development of capitalism in backward countries are found in classical studies of imperialism. The English liberal J. A. Hobson, in *Imperialism* (1902), stressed domestic underconsumption as the cause of British imperialist expansion to other parts of the world. In *Das Finanzkapital* (1910), Rudolf Hilferding emphasized finance capital as the basis of the monopoly phase of capitalism. In *The Accumulation of Capital* (1913), Rosa Luxemburg offered one of the most complete early analyses of the impact of imperialism on backward countries. In *Imperialism and World Economy* (1915), N. I. Bukharin looked at the process of integration of national economies into a world economy, although he did not delve into the consequences of imperialism for backward countries. In 1916, Lenin examined the economic changes in the advanced countries of the capitalist system, in particular the role of international capital and the tendency of capitalism to evolve toward its monopoly or imperialist stage. His *Development of Capitalism in Russia* (1899) has been called "his most important study of the development of capitalism in a backward nation . . . the pioneering classic of dependency studies" (Palma 1978, 890).

Gabriel Palma points out that Lenin's early work on Russia emanated from debates about the necessity and possibility of capitalist development in that country. The Narodniks argued that capitalist development was neither necessary nor viable for Russia to evolve toward socialism; they believed that the capitalist stage could be skipped altogether. Lenin countered that Russia, although backward in contrast to other capitalist countries, was in fact capitalist. Commenting on the stages of capitalist development in Russian industry, Lenin wrote:

> There are three main stages in this development: small commodity-production (small, mainly peasant industries); capitalist manufacture; and the factory (large-scale machine industry). . . . The connection and continuity between the forms of industry mentioned is of the most direct and intimate kind. The facts quite clearly show that the main trend of small commodity-production is towards the development of capitalism, and in particular, towards the rise of manufacture. [Lenin 1956, 594–595]

According to Palma, a significant contribution Lenin made to the study of capitalist development in backward nations was his analysis of the slowness of Russian development in comparison with that of other capitalist nations. He attributed this to a weak bourgeoisie, competition from Western Europe, and the resiliency of the traditional structures in Russia. Palma suggests that these obstacles to the growth of capitalism in Russia might be characterized by contemporary writers as "the development of Russian underdevelopment" (Palma 1978, 892). Lenin showed the ties between the different modes of production existing in Russia at the turn of the century, demonstrating, for example, that handicraft industry could not be separated from factory industry. He held that capitalism was politically necessary and economically feasible; that capitalist development was already under way in Russia;

that capitalist development in backward nations was not simply a process of breaking down the precapitalist structures but "a more complex process of interplay between internal and external structures" involving traditional structures as well; and that eventually, capitalist development and the bourgeois-democratic revolution associated with it would attain the level of development of Western Europe (Palma 1978, 893).

Palma says that the revolution of 1905 and the collapse of the Second International apparently convinced Lenin and his comrades, including Trotsky, that they must modify their position regarding the necessity of full capitalist development. They saw in the 1905 revolution the possibility of allowing the proletariat to carry out the process of completing the bourgeois-democratic revolution. They also understood that Russia might be a weak link in the struggle against capitalism and would advance more rapidly toward socialism with the help of more-developed socialist societies. Palma believes that although this analysis of Lenin must not be applied mechanically to other periods and regions of the world, Lenin does offer a path:

> This is the study of the concrete forms of articulation between the
> capitalist sectors of the backward nations and the advanced nations
> in the system, and of the concrete forms taken by the subordination
> of pre-capitalist forms of production to the former, and to the rest
> of the system. It is essentially the study of the dynamic of the
> backward nations as a synthesis of the general determinants of the
> capitalist system (external factors) and the specific determinants of
> each (internal factors). [Palma 1978, 895]

Palma concludes that Lenin and other theorists of his time had recognized that imperialism could deter capitalist development in the backward countries but felt that once the bonds of colonialism had been broken, there would be a possibility of advancing. Thus the classical writers on imperialism assumed that with such a break, capitalism could be progressive in backward countries. Russia, however, was never a colony of a Western European power, and Latin America, despite its independence, fell under the yoke of North American imperialism. The struggle against imperialism, according to Palma, is the struggle for industrialization and autonomous capitalist development.

Trotsky

Trotsky resided in exile in Mexico from 1937 until his assassination in 1940, and his ideas had a profound impact on, for example, the Bolivian

Revolution of 1952, the peasant uprising in Peru and the rural guerrilla movements in Guatemala during the early sixties, and the urban guerrilla movement in Argentina a decade later.[20] The essence of Trotskyism is found in his *Permanent Revolution* ([1930] 1962) and *The Russian Revolution* ([1932] 1959), both written after his opposition to Stalin's policy of promoting socialism in one country, beginning in 1923, and his expulsion from the Soviet Communist party in 1927.

The Trotskyist understanding of development can be traced, first, to Trotsky's theory of permanent revolution, which he believed was drawn from Marx:

> The permanent revolution, in the sense which Marx attached to this concept, means a revolution which makes no compromise with any single form of class rule, which does not stop at the democratic stage, which goes over to socialist measures and to war against reaction from without; that is, a revolution whose every successive stage is rooted in the preceding one and which can and only in complete liquidation of class society. [Trotsky 1964, 62]

Trotsky opposed efforts to establish and maintain the reformist democratic stage, arguing that "the democratic tasks of the backward bourgeois nations led directly, in our epoch, to the dictatorship of the proletariat and that dictatorship of the proletariat puts socialist tasks on the order of the day." Thus the democratic stage is merely transitional, and the socialist reconstruction of society will be the direct consequence of "a permanent state of revolutionary development" (Trotsky 1964, 63–64). He considered the socialist revolution part of an ongoing process in which each stage of transformation emerges from the preceding stage and all social relations undergo change. In his view, the socialist revolution begins on a national level but inevitably spreads to other countries, in particular the advanced ones: "A national revolution is not a self-contained whole; it is only a link in the international chain" (Trotsky 1964, 65).

A second element in Trotsky's conception of development and underdevelopment relates to what he called the law of uneven and combined development. In the early pages of *History and the Russian Revolution*, he argued that backward countries do not necessarily follow the path of the advanced capitalist countries. Their path is not predetermined. Indeed, they may skip stages en route to socialism: "Their development as a whole acquires a planless, complex, combined character" (Trotsky 1959, 3).

> Unevenness, the most general law of the historic process, reveals itself most sharply and complexly in the destiny of the backward

countries. Under the whip of external necessity their backward culture is compelled to make leaps. From the universal law of unevenness thus derives another law which, for the lack of a better name, we may call the law of *combined development*—by which we mean a drawing together of the different stages of the journey, a combining of separate steps, an amalgam of archaic with more contemporary forms. [Trotsky 1959, 4]

These ideas opposed Stalin's theory of revolution through stages, a process in which a democratic revolution in backward nations would occur independent of a proletarian revolution. They also countered Stalin's emphasis on the possibility of socialism in one country, Russia. On the latter position, Trotsky cited Lenin's concern about Russia's "subordination" to the international market: "Anyone who sees in the admission of our dependence on the world market (Lenin spoke directly of our SUBORDINATION to the world market) . . . reveals thereby his own provincial petty-bourgeois feebleness in the face of the world market" (Trotsky 1929, 53).

Trotsky argued that socialism depends largely on the outcome of a world revolution. Thus proletarian revolutions must spread to the advanced countries, and backward countries may be the first to establish a proletarian revolution but the last to reach socialism. Backward countries, in the process of establishing a proletarian revolution, must develop the forces of production in the struggle to establish socialism.

In summary, Marx anticipated current thinking on development and underdevelopment with his observation that capitalism may be both regressive and progressive in backward countries—progressive where industrial capital has devastated the precapitalist social formations, leaving in its wake the material conditions for the foundation for an advancing capitalism, and regressive where merchant capital undermines the precapitalist social formations without necessarily transforming the old social formations and generating the new divisions of labor that are representative of industrial capitalism today. With his emphasis on relations of production, Marx also demonstrated the importance of class analysis.

Lenin elaborated on the idea, inherent in Marx, that an international division of labor can lead to dominant industrial and dependent agricultural parts of the world. In his study of capitalist development in Russia, Lenin demonstrated that even in a backward nation capitalism was under way, and most important, he showed that different modes of production were evident in Russia. Before the Russian Revolution, Lenin insisted on the necessity of capitalist development in the advance toward socialism. However, the rise of social democracy in Europe and the more rapid and successful revolutionary process in Russia made it clear that the path to socialism could be speeded up. The establishment of bourgeois democracy was but a brief transitional phase in the revolution, and the proletariat could be given a chance to come to power.

Many of these ideas in Marx and Lenin were compatible with the thinking of Trotsky, who advocated permanent revolution throughout the world and the coming to power of the proletariat in backward countries. Stages could be skipped in this revolutionary process, but only the rise of the proletariat in the advanced countries would eventually allow for socialism in the backward areas. Trotsky agreed with Lenin that various modes of production could exist at the same time in backward nations like Russia, and he recognized that dependency on the world market undermined the prospects for geniune socialism in a given country.

3 / Capitalism and the Nationalist and Reformist Tradition

After the Second World War, concern began to be expressed in Latin America about the domination of advanced nations such as Great Britain and the United States, Britain especially in Argentina and Chile at the turn of the century and the United States there and elsewhere after 1930. Nationalist sentiment frequently turned against these outside powers with an outcry against imperialism, a demand that national resources be preserved, and insistence that the domestic economy be transformed through capitalism, but autonomously as the U.S. economy itself had once been transformed. These ideas were promoted through the writings of a group of economists associated with ECLA, established in 1948, and three personalities stand out: Raúl Prebisch, Osvaldo Sunkel, and Celso Furtado. Mention should also be made of François Perroux and his followers. Within this tendency, new directions were taken by Pablo González Casanova and Fernando Henrique Cardoso.

Origins

Center and Periphery: Prebisch

Raúl Prebisch was born in 1901 in Tucumán, graduated in economics from the University of Buenos Aires, and later worked for both the university and the government of Argentina. From 1935 to 1943 he served as head of the Central Bank; in 1948 he was involved in the establishment of ECLA and eventually became its director.

Essentially, Prebisch divided the world into two parts, a center of industrialized countries and a periphery of underdeveloped countries. He seems to have accepted that the relationship between industrialized and underdeveloped countries could benefit both, but, according to Werner Baer, he did not believe that unrestrained consumption could have this result. He believed that long-term deterioration in the terms of trade in the periphery caused by distortions in international demand and supply would impede development there as capital goods and other manufactured imports became expensive and exchange earnings declined (Baer 1969). The solution to this disparity would be indus-trialization accompanied by tariff protection against high-cost imports, the objective being to preserve and enhance the people's standard of living by preventing the transfer of income to the center and sheltering domestic industry. The state would have to build a base or infrastructure upon which industry could arise—power, roads, raw materials, and the means whereby domestic industry could support itself.

According to Joseph Love, a theory of unequal exchange was emerging in the thought of Prebisch as early as 1937: "Manufacturing industries, and therefore industrial nations, can efficaciously control production, thereby maintaining the value of their products at desired levels. This is not the case with agricultural and livestock countries" (*Revista Económica,* ser. 2, no. 1 [1937], 26–27, quoted in Love 1980, 52). In addition, the *Revista* suggested that autonomous, not export-oriented, growth had occurred during the worldwide depression of 1929–1936 and would be a viable path toward economic development. Prebisch apparently first referred to "center" and "periphery" in lectures during 1944 (interview cited in Love 1980, 52). At the same time, he also referred to the idea of inward-directed development, which later would be employed to describe the ECLA *desarrollista,* or develop-mentalist approach.[21] The hegemony of the United States, he believed, characterized that country's relationship with Argentina and other parts of the backward world.

In May 1949, in response to a resolution of ECLA calling for a study of the terms of trade in Latin America, Prebisch elaborated his ideas about deterioration of terms of trade.[22] He argued that from the late nineteenth century to the Second World War, prices had favored exporters of industrial goods in advanced capitalist countries over exporters of agricultural goods and raw materials in peripheral countries. He particularly noted the negative impact on prices of downward trends in trade cycles. ECLA criticized the international division of labor and urged the industrialization of the periphery as a solution to disparities in development between center and periphery. Protection of the prices of raw materials, especially during downturns in trade cycles, was essential to this approach.

Joseph Love sees four basic sources for the doctrines of Prebisch and ECLA (Love 1980, 60–65). One is classical mercantilist theory and policies that encouraged industrialization in the interests of the nation. Among these policies was the implementation of tariffs to protect domestic industry, and a spokesman for such a position was Alejandro Bunge, an Argentine proponent of industrialization during the 1920s. A second source is the writings of economists of countries in central and Eastern Europe. During the depression of the thirties, writers such as N. Kaldor and P. N. Rosenstein-Rodan advocated manufacturing to correct the imbalance caused by solely agricultural exports and underdevelopment. The Romanian Mihail Manoilesco apparently anticipated many of the arguments of ECLA. Manoilesco, a central banker like Prebisch, urged protectionism in his attack on the disparities between the industrial countries and the backward agricultural countries, and his ideas were used to build the theoretical foundations of corporatism in Portugal and other fascist nations during the thirties. Capitalism and fascism promoted the idea of a third position between capitalism and socialism, but the corporate systems that emerged could best be described as oriented toward autonomous capitalist development.[23] A fourth possible source is the work of the German Werner Sombart, who as early as 1928 wrote about the capitalist center and peripheral nations and described the dependency between them (Sombart, cited in Love 1980, 71 n. 77).

Prebisch has written recently that although he was once influenced by nineteenth-century neoclassical theories, today he recognizes that such theories, along with the ideas of Marx and Keynes, have little relevance to any analysis of what he calls the development of peripheral capitalism (Prebisch 1978). Oriented toward a "global" interpretation and toward the study of influences of capitalist centers on peripheral capitalism, he discounts the idea that capitalism in the periphery will simply reproduce the capitalism of the centers. He argues that the periphery has suffered a historical delay in its capitalist development, owing to the hegemony of the centers, especially over technology, means of consumption, cultural forms, and ideologies. The result has been a social structure in the periphery that is different from that of the centers. He suggests that the underconsumption of the substantial portion of the population that is unable to benefit from capitalist development is a consequence, not of capitalism itself, but of a social structure that permits income to concentrate in the hands of the people who own and control the majority of the means of production and that relegates a large part of the working population to low levels of productivity. Capital accumulation is insufficient to absorb all of the work force; even though there is constant accumulation, it is diverted to higher strata that imitate the forms of consumption of the centers, and the portion of the work force that is absorbed lacks the skills and technology that are characteristic of workers in the centers.

Prebisch sees a tendency toward conflict between the upper strata of "social power" and the lower strata of "union and political power," moderated by intermediary strata oriented toward democratization that emerge as technology penetrates industry and other activities. Other contradictions in the relations between center and periphery include the fact that there is no spontaneous expansion of the center's capitalism in the periphery. Rather, industrialization of the periphery has been a deliberate process resulting from successive crises in the centers that have required that large firms from those centers and, more recently, multinationals penetrate the periphery. Further, the periphery suffers from financial arrangements that bring it not only capital but also disequilibrium. Also, the periphery is excluded from the exchange of industrial goods that benefits the centers. Neither the neoclassicists nor the Marxists have been able to understand the periphery's capacity for imitative capitalism. The capitalist process in the periphery differs substantially from that of the centers. Prebisch looks to a grand synthesis of liberal and socialist ideas: The state, he argues, must assume a primary role in determining the pace of accumulation, but it is not necessary to transfer the means of production to the state in order to achieve this objective.

Prebisch links this theory of peripheral capitalism to dependency. Peripheral capitalism in Latin America is oriented toward a privileged consumer society and thus excludes the masses. "The process of capital accumulation and the introduction of new technologies from industrial centres are not motivated by the purpose of progressively incorporating new social strata into the development process" (Prebisch 1980, 21). The notion that the periphery can reproduce in a form approximating that of the centers is wrong.

> I would characterize this peripheral capitalism of ours as a phe-
> nomenon arising from irradiation by the technologies of the industrial
> centres, and consisting of forms of consumption, institutions, ideas,
> and ideologies characteristic of a purely imitative capitalism. . . .
> Such reproduction is not possible due to the contradictions which
> these phenomena of propagation and irradiation bring about in the
> social structure of the periphery. . . . Capital accumulation, in turn,
> is incompatible with the spread of the consumer society. [Prebisch
> 1980, 21]

The insufficiency of accumulation is related to surplus and relations of the periphery with the centers. These relations are defined by dependence.

> By dependence I mean the relations between centres and the pe-
> riphery whereby a country is subjected to decisions taken in the
> centres, not only in economic matters, but also in matters of politics
> and strategy for domestic and foreign policies. The consequence is
> that due to exterior pressure the country cannot decide autono-
> mously what it should do or cease doing. The structural changes

bring about an awareness of this phenomenon, and this awareness, this desire for autonomy, is one of the integral elements in a critical understanding of the system. [Prebisch 1980, 25]

The Prebisch approach clearly moves toward an autonomous capitalist solution. The state must assume a dominant role, but rather than socialize the means of production, it must work to coordinate private and public enterprise in order to overcome the obstacles and contradictions between center and periphery. This solution, as Baer insists (1969, 217–218), is not really a challenge to the classical theory of international trade but allows for analysis where the classical theory offered little contribution. Prebisch does refute the classical assumption of competition and shows the differences between capitalism in the center and capitalism in the periphery. He seeks to understand how the underdeveloped nations can adjust to international conditions through government intervention in the form of subsidy, tariff protection, or import substitution. In this way, the periphery may be able to find a means to offset the effects of the hegemonic centers.

Poles of Development: Perroux and Andrade

The French economist François Perroux proposed a solution to the problem of underdevelopment involving well-planned multinational investment and the overcoming of such obstacles as insufficient capitalist diffusion from the industrial centers to outlying regions and rural areas. Although his writing concentrated on development in Europe,[24] he also wrote about Latin America. At least one Latin American social scientist, Manuel Correia de Andrade, has been influenced by his ideas.

Perroux argued that both neoclassical theory—dealing with the supply and demand for savings, marginal productivity, and so on—and Keynesian theory were irrelevant to the situation. Instead, he advocated an analysis of development poles, areas, and axes. He defined a development pole as an entrepreneurial activity or a "motor unit interlinked with its surrounding environment" (Perroux 1968, 103). The idea is that the economic activities of a new enterprise are integrated into and linked with the economy of a region or country. Growth is understood as sustained increase, for example, in the gross product, whereas development involves production related to needs of a population. A development pole is located in an outlying area, but it should be tied to the regional or national economy; that is, there should be a link with the primary processing of raw materials as well as with an enterprise oriented toward domestic producers and consumers. When several development poles are interrelated, a development area is evident.

"Newly opened-up lands, physical and intellectual infrastructures and irrigation and other improvement works together constitute an environment suited to the birth of development poles, which in turn act upon that environment" (Perroux 1968, 108). Development axes consist of systems of development poles, exemplified in France by the Mont Blanc tunnel.

Perroux identified four basic effects of development poles and areas: investment, product, income, and balance of trade. He related these effects to integration patterns involving multinational firms and the region or country represented by development poles and areas. He suggested policy direction toward resolving the difficulties of the development task and the extreme regional inequalities within the countries of Latin America. He expressed sympathy for the position of building national integration prior to international integration, which, he said,

> finds some support in the desirability of bringing about internal cohesion of the production apparatus, of developing certain sections of very backward countries and, in the final analysis, of intermeshing the production apparatus and the population. . . . integration offers the means for optimum and rapid achievement: it is one of the motor forces of expansion, it avoids duplication of capital investment, and it facilitates diffusion of the most modern technologies and of the latest innovations. [Perroux 1968, 124]

Further, he said, such integration would allow a nation to develop and also ensure the right of peoples to self-determination and control over development poles.

This approach was applied to northeastern Brazil by the Brazilian geographer and economist Manuel Correia de Andrade. His major contributions were a synthesis of theories and ideas in the European literature on the subject and an analysis of various cycles of economic development familiar to the historical experience of Brazil: for example, sugarcane in the Northeast, gold and the development of Rio de Janeiro, cotton in São Luiz do Maranhão, coffee in the Southeast, and rubber in the Amazon region. Andrade also offered an analysis of industrialization and the formation of a national pole of development. He suggested that whatever progress had occurred was conditioned by the dependency of one pole upon another; for example, in the cases of Recife, Salvador, and Rio in the past and São Paulo today in their relations with Europe and the United States. He concluded that this development had not resulted in an internal market capable of sustaining itself and that production was largely destined for export, but he expressed hope that development could be brought about through establishment of regional poles of development. In particular, he identified the satellite cities of Recife as examples. The Pernambuco state government had attempted to establish an industrial district in Cabo between 1959 and 1964, and during the late sixties, the Superintendencia do Desenvolvimento do Nordeste (SUDENE) had studied the possibility that the interior urban center of Juàzeiro and Petrolina could emerge as a pole of development (Andrade 1967).

The poles-of-development approach was designed to confront the inequity between centers and peripheries and to mitigate the negative impact of dependent relationships through the introduction of central planning. Identification of potential poles of development, establishment of an infrastructure of resources involving power and transportation and other considerations, and investment for new industry were considered early steps in the process of building an integrated economic center. Rational diffusion of capital and technology to the isolated centers would, it was believed, ensure their emergence as autonomous areas of development. At the same time, it was considered necessary to link these centers into an integrated national scheme of development, to establish national control, and to ensure a balance in regard to international investment and involvement.

Dominance and Dependence: Sunkel

Osvaldo Sunkel, a Chilean economist once closely associated with ECLA, identified the structure of foreign trade—raw-material exports and manufactured imports—as the cause of the instability, stagnation, deteriorating terms of trade, and other problems that affect underdeveloped countries (see Sunkel 1972). Dependency, he believed, links the development of the international capitalist system to the processes of development and underdevelopment within a society.[25] Thus foreign influences must be examined, not as external, but as internal effects. Usually the consequence is "a self-reinforcing accumulation of privilege for special groups as well as the continued existence of a marginal class" (Sunkel 1972, 519). Sunkel saw the nation-state as a subsystem of an international capitalist system. Underdevelopment for him was not necessarily simply a result of the economic, political, and cultural isolation of a society; underdevelopment and development were simultaneous processes representing "the two faces of the historical evolution of the capitalist system" (Sunkel 1972, 520). He illustrated this proposition by reference to the historical experiences of the old and new centers of the capitalist world—Europe, Japan, and the United States—and their impact on Latin America. He focused attention especially on the multinational firm and the crisis it has fomented through its massive penetration of local economies, the introduction of highly capital-intensive technology, and the promotion of consumption capitalism. Often the result is the destruction or co-optation of national capital and entrepreneurs, thereby depriving the society of autonomous development. The dependency and marginalization that inevitably occur, he believed, are being dealt with by a process of dependent state capitalism. In this process, an increasing share of the ownership and control of natural resources is given to foreign firms while the state apparatus provides the infrastructure to facilitate their investment and expansion. This process of denationalization leads to increasing inequality. An example of this tendency is Brazil, where the ruling classes have accepted these conditions.

In contrast to the Brazilian example, other countries, such as Peru under Juan Velasco Alvarado and Chile under Salvador Allende, reacted by attempting to gain control over their economies. In Peru, nationalist elements in the military took over the apparatuses of the state, while in Chile, such a takeover was accomplished partially through the electoral process. Sunkel argued that such developments must be accompanied by three reformist measures: change in the agrarian structure, use of primary exports to finance expansion of heavy and consumer industries, and reorganization of industry away from conspicuous consumption of the minority and toward the satisfaction of the basic needs of the majority of the people. For Sunkel, the objective was clearly reformist, nationalist, and autonomous capitalist development:

> What we are seeing is the assertion of the national interest of our countries in their international economic relations. The aim is greater autonomy, in order to achieve development without "dependencia" and without marginalization. To achieve this goal, the asymmetrical nature of the present system of international economic relations must first undergo a thorough reform. [Sunkel 1972, 531]

Sunkel suggested that his conception of development and underdevelopment leads to the recognition of two dichotomies. The first is a division of the world into developed, industrialized, advanced, "central northern" countries and underdeveloped, poor, dependent, "peripheral southern" countries. The second is the polarization within countries of advanced, modern groups and regions and backward, primitive ones. This approach thus directs attention to both an international and a national level of analysis, and it relates study to "partial but independent structures, which form part of a single whole": a developed dominant structure and an underdeveloped dependent one (Sunkel 1970, 6-7).

External Dependence: Furtado

The Brazilian economist Celso Furtado was born in 1920 in Pombal, Paraiba, and graduated in law from the University of Brazil and in economics from the University of Paris. He joined ECLA in 1949 and there prepared studies on a development program for Brazil. Later, as director of the Banco Nacional de Desenvolvimento Econômico, he elaborated plans for the economic recovery of northeastern Brazil. As head of the SUDENE, the agency empowered with carrying out development schemes in the Northeast, Furtado exercised considerable influence over the regional planning process. His ideas about development and underdevelopment evolved through a dozen or so books, the most important, *The Economic Growth of Brazil,* being a historical analysis of Brazil since the arrival of the Portuguese (see Furtado 1959, 1963).

In his overview, Furtado stressed the commercial capitalist influence of the Portuguese in Brazil, especially through the sugar industry and the slave trade. In his analysis of the expansion of the economy of the Northeast during the sixteenth and seventeenth centuries, he portrayed the rise and decline of the sugar industry and the cattle breeding activity that accompanied it. He concluded that the slow decline of the sugar industry had contributed to the subsistence economy that characterized the population and to problems in later periods: "In this way the Brazilian Northeast became converted from a high-productivity economic system into an economy in which the major part of the population produced only what was necessary for its bare existence. Dispersion of a part of the population through extensive cattle breeding caused an involution in the division of labor and specialization, resulting in a reversion to primitive techniques, even in craftsmanship activities" (Furtado 1963, 70-71).

This perspective on Brazilian history suggests the underlying explanation of development and underdevelopment that runs through the work of Furtado. In one treatment of these terms, Furtado traced the evolution of classical and Marxist thought on questions of capitalist accumulation, especially in Europe. He identified three ways in which Europe disrupted the world economy in the eighteenth century and thereafter: disorganization of the precapitalist artisan economy, displacement of borders wherever there was unoccupied land, and expansion and penetration into inhabited but precapitalist areas. The consequence of this activity was the formation of "hybrid structures," some functioning as part of the capitalist system, and others, within the previous system, with its precapitalist features. He called this a dualistic economy and argued that underdevelopment was a "discrete historical process through which economies that have already achieved a high level of development have not necessarily passed" (Furtado 1964, 129). This perspective does not imply that a precapitalist character is associated with the backward structures of a society in all cases; for example, in Brazil, a good portion of wages was connected with the international market. Underdevelopment, Furtado argued, is part of a process caused by the "penetration of modern capitalistic enterprise into archaic structures" (Furtado 1964, 138). In contemporary Brazil, foreign companies producing export commodities exist alongside sub-sistence activities while an industrial nucleus connected with the domestic market develops through the displacement of imported cap-italist goods. Industrialization in underdeveloped economies is thus oriented toward the replacement of imports with local products, but "investment can lead to the creation of unemployment in spite of the existence of large, underemployed masses both within the monetary economy and outside it," which is "why the economics of present-day underdeveloped structures are not very dynamic and have strong internal tendencies toward stagnation" (Furtado 1965, 61).

Furtado also examined the social structure of the underdeveloped economy. At the top, he saw a ruling class composed of various interest groups, usually antagonistic to each other and therefore unable to agree on a plan for national development. These groups include the original landowners, who are connected to foreign trade, in favor of free trade, and opposed to interference of the state; capitalists who support free trade but rely on the state apparatuses to ensure foreign trade; and capitalists supported by the internal market, who are protectionist and use the state to manipulate resources for their own benefit. Below the ruling class is a mass of salaried urban workers employed in services, a class of industrial workers, and at the bottom, a class of peasants. Furtado argued that struggle among these classes is usually absent in underdeveloped countries because class consciousness is low and working-class ideology is not clearly formulated. In Brazil, for instance, inflation distorts and obscures any identification with the class struggle, as employers are more likely to grant wage increases than to oppose strikers because the consumer ultimately pays for the increases (Furtado 1965, 61).

These political and economic considerations led Furtado to the position that transplanting consumption patterns through import sub-stitution and industrialization at home gives rise to peripheral capitalism. Peripheral capitalism is unable to generate innovation and depends on outside decisions to transform the local economy. This situation he called external dependence.

External dependence results in a self-sustaining process of underdevelopment in certain countries, according to Furtado. He elaborated on this idea both in economic and political terms.

> What always accompanies the rise in economic productivity is the transplantation of new consumption patterns, namely, the modernization of the way of life of a small minority of the population. During the period of industrialization based on import substitution, the external demand for primary products no longer plays a dynamic role in transforming the dependent economies. The assimilation of technical progress feeds the process of growth for a time, but once the substitution process exhausts its main possibilities, the dynamic role has to be assumed by the new products produced domestically for the rich minority. This is possible only if the dimensions of the economy allow a full process of industrialization and if the political system is repressive enough to maintain income concentration. [Furtado 1973, 121]

Thus external dependence and underdevelopment tend to persist through various stages of development. In an early stage, an increase in exports of raw materials benefits a wealthy minority, which adapts its consumption patterns to the values of countries in the center. In a more advanced stage, import substitution may stimulate some internal development, but only temporarily. Ultimately, full industrialization might solve the problem, but here, too, underdevelopment has tended to perpetuate itself under peripheral capitalism, especially in the face of the imbalance in the international system brought about by activities of multinational corporations that reap the benefits of increased productivity in dependent economies. Furtado concluded:

> This process does not avoid an increasing disparity in the productivity levels of the center and the periphery, and it implies a widening gap between the consumption levels of the modernized minorities and the mass of the population in the dependent countries . . . from the point of view of the underdeveloped countries, growth will continue to thwart their efforts at overcoming dependence, improving living conditions, and reducing inequalities within their societies. [Furtado 1973, 122–123; see 1971 for a similar discussion]

Furtado illustrated his thesis by referring to many situations in Latin America (see Furtado 1970, 1978), but he gave the greatest amount of attention to Brazil. Since the end of the Second World War, economists have emphasized the developmental potential of Brazil, with its vast natural resources. After the military coup of 1964, many observers devoted attention to the growth of the Brazilian economy in the face of inflation and other persistent problems. During the late sixties and early seventies, the military regime proclaimed that an economic "miracle" had occurred, a claim that was largely discredited by the international petroleum crisis in 1973 and ensuing events. In a recent work, Furtado (1981) has exposed the myth of the miracle, at the same time imploring Brazilians to recognize the impact of underdevelopment and the malformations of their society. Arguing a familiar line, Furtado points to the "interests" behind the fundamental political problems and the outside technology that affects the style of life and disguises the reality of contradictions and inequality. Finally, he is optimistic: Brazil, he feels, can assume the role in the Third World of challenging the international order as forces within the country evolve in a direction "favoring those who suffer from dependence and exploitation" (Furtado 1981, 89).

Furtado, Prebisch, and Sunkel shared a structural approach in which capitalist centers were distinguishable from peripheral areas, and they tended to examine underdevelopment by reference to terms of trade. Prebisch looked at the negative impact of prices during cycles of economic activity. He gave his analysis a global interpretation but discounted neoclassical and Marxist approaches. He attributed the internal contradictions in the periphery to the underconsumption of a large part of the population and to the concentration of income in the hands of the owners of the means of production. He concluded that there was insufficient capital accumulation in the periphery to absorb all of the work force.

Sunkel agreed that accumulation tends to be directed toward special groups. He saw dependency and marginalization as reflections of dependent state capitalism and the activity of the multinationals. He suggested that a solution to these problems might be found in reformist measures such as agrarian reform, utilization of primary exports to finance industrialization, and a reorganization of industry away from the consumption demands of the ruling minority.

Furtado identified capitalist disruptions in Europe to illustrate the appearance of hybrid structures and dualistic economies in the periphery. He also related the structure of social classes to peripheral capitalism and external dependence. With Prebisch and Sunkel, Furtado attributed these conditions to the consumption patterns of a wealthy minority. He argued that underdevelopment tends to prevail under peripheral capitalism and that the solution might be found in central planning to promote autonomous capitalism. (Perroux also advocated this solution, though stressing multinational rather than local investment.)

Whereas Prebisch believed that import substitution and industrialization could allow for autonomous, national, and capitalist development, Sunkel and Furtado recognized the limitations of this approach, both in theory and experience. Thus Sunkel concentrated attention on other reforms as well, and Furtado emphasized central planning. All three analyzed the deforming character of outside capital, but Sunkel and Furtado pointed out that capitalism cannot reproduce itself in the periphery so as to serve the needs of the majority of the people.

New Directions

Internal Colonialism: González Casanova

The Mexican social scientist Pablo González Casanova, the son of a wealthy landowning family in Yucatán, was born in 1922. His father was a linguist and student of Indian languages, and this academic orientation seems to have influenced the younger Pablo to pursue his own academic career.[26] He earned a master's degree in history and then spent three years in Paris studying sociology and philosophy, especially the thought of Hegel and French existentialism, and writing a thesis on French ideology with regard to Latin America under the supervision of Fernand Braudel.[27] He was especially interested in how "Europeans in various epochs saw America in terms of their own changing perspectives, such as the need for a utopia, and projected those ideas onto the American reality whether they corresponded or not."[28] After returning to Mexico, González Casanova joined the faculty and later the administration of the national university, serving as rector in 1970-1972. He writing and thought can be organized in terms of works focused on Mexico and its development or lack of development, on Latin American history and the impact of imperialism, and on concepts and methodology in the social sciences.

His analysis of Mexico—presented, for the most part, in his classic study *Democracy in Mexico* (1970a)—is both theoretical and factual. He is concerned with the structure of power, the relationship of social and economic structures, and the effect on political decisions of economic development. In dealing with these themes, González Casanova adopts an eclectic approach, drawing upon both Marxism and contemporary social science but rejecting crude empiricism and dogmatism. He sees Mexico as evolving through a precapitalist stage, influenced by imperialism and the victim of internal colonialism. He favors growth in terms of income as well as distribution of resources among the people.

He hopes for a peaceful transition from welfare capitalism to democratic socialism, guided by the state and a strong national bourgeoisie.[29]

González Casanova identifies an official hierarchical concentration of power located in the dominant party, the Partido Revolucionario Institucional (PRI). In coordination with the presidency and the executive branch, the PRI has gradually consolidated power on all levels by isolating local bosses, or caciques, placing constraints on the military, and limiting the influence of the church. Although the large industrialists and financiers have succeeded in establishing a power base outside this official hierarchy, they are also subject to regulations and constraints imposed by the state. The appearance, then, is of a polity characterized by competing elite groups or bases of power. Given this structure of power, the Mexican Revolution has achieved great progress, including peace and stability, a mixed economy of state-guided capitalism, and some growth.

Despite these accomplishments, Mexico continues to struggle against foreign capitalist influence. In 1938, there was the Mexican takeover of the petroleum industry; later the government purchased foreign power utilities and maintained diplomatic ties with the revolutionary governments in Cuba and Nicaragua. The state has become the country's largest entrepreneur and provides the possibility of a rational utilization of resources within a free enterprise economy. The state attempts to control external pressures, negotiates with the large monopolies, and promotes national development.

Although imperialism is more or less contained, an internal colonialism similar to the colonial relationship between nations is evident within Mexico. Certain regions, classes, and groups exist in a marginal situation. This marginal society, composed generally of Indians, is exploited by and dependent on a dominant society of Spanish, Creoles, and Ladinos. The relationship between these two societies is dualist: one society dominates and exploits the other; one is participant, the other isolated. The cultural alignment of dominant and dominated peoples reflects racial prejudice and discrimination as well as other colonial forms of exploitation and control.

In considering how to resolve this problem, González Casanova offers two solutions, one from a Marxist perspective and the other from the viewpoint of contemporary mainstream sociology. Citing Marx, Lenin, and other radical thinkers, González Casanova argues that after the Mexican Revolution, a compromise was reached between factions and classes that resulted in a liberal constitution and some social rights, but in effect, the constitution was an instrument of the emerging bourgeoisie in alliance with the organized workers and armed peasants who were struggling against imperialism. Mexico is precapitalist and predemocratic in the sense that neither a capitalist system nor a fully bourgeois government has been established. The country will not, he believes, experience another revolution until the present social structure has proved obsolete. For one thing, no country that has experienced a bourgeois-democratic revolution and gone through a period of cap- italist development has yet had a socialist revolution; for another, the masses must unify with the bourgeoisie against imperialism and on behalf of capitalist democracy and peaceful development at the same time as they organize as a class themselves:

> The development of class consciousness and of a class for itself— the integration of a true proletarian organization—can be realized only through the tactics of alliance and struggle with the national bourgeoisie and of internal democratization of working-class and peasant organizations. . . . There must be a permanent confirmation of the anti-imperialist pact with the bourgeoisie, continuous educa- tion of the working class about the forms of struggle, and recognition that the working class has a national task to fulfill—namely, a dem- ocratic task. [González Casanova 1970a, 172]

González Casanova goes on to stress that whether the national bour- geoisie supports a nationalist or a Marxist revolution, it can be counted on to lead the capitalist development of the country. Thus an alliance of the proletariat with such a progressive capitalist class could lead to the elimination of precapitalist forms of production and, eventually, to the peaceful development of socialism. If, on the other hand, "the development of capitalism is suspended, the democratic organization of the working class is permanently impeded, and imperialist and domestic reaction triumph," then socialism will not be achieved peace- fully (González Casanova 1970a, 177).

González Casanova shifts his attention to a sociological view of the revolution, departing from Tocqueville and referring to the thought of Max Weber, Seymour Martin Lipset, and Ralf Dahrendorf. He argues that the prospects for democracy are greater today than in the past, although obstacles persist. In modernizing its economy, he believes that Mexico will acquire the characteristics of advanced industrial societies oriented toward institutionalization of conflict and achievement of democracy. Thus this view of the revolution is much like that of some Marxists.[30] Through capitalist development, a bourgeois democracy will evolve, and national integration, stability, and harmony will be achieved. "Sociological analysis can tell us only that the development of democracy in Mexico is within the realm of the probable, owing to the over-all level of development in the country, and that effective democracy is the indispensable prerequisite for continued peaceful development" (González Casanova 1970a, 192).

González Casanova attempts to place this emphasis on development and underdevelopment into a theoretical context in a series of essays on the sociology of exploitation (González Casanova 1970b), in which he tries to reconcile the differences between North American empirical investigation and the historical models of Marxism. Kahl has commented that this effort is that of "one who stands between two powerful traditions claiming his allegiance and who seeks to understand them both in order to choose that which is useful from each without succumbing to a superficial eclecticism" (Kahl 1976, 97). On the empirical side, González Casanova concludes that most research does not measure exploitation because this concept is considered to be ideological rather than scientific. Further, a concept such as development is usually used by empiricists to imply a desired direction and progress, a tendency that ignores the cyclical experience of capitalism. In fact, he argues, empiricism itself is ideological and unscientific to the extent that it renounces the scientific study of its own values (interview cited in Kahl 1976, 99). Marxism in its vulgar form also lacks scientific precision, since the concept of exploitation may be used to explain everything without any effort to relate it to factors such as changes in the forces of production or to specify and analyze the historical context (Kahl 1976, 100).

González Casanova approaches the study of internal colonialism in two ways: "one which allows the typification of colonialism as an integral phenomenon, changeable from an international to an internal category; and another which permits us to see how the phenomenon has occurred in a new nation which has reached the 'takeoff stage' " (González Casanova, in Horowitz, Castro, and Gerassi 1969, 121).[31] He begins by defining "colony" as a territory without self-government, in an unequal position in relation to the metropolis, dominated by another state, and so on. He shows that the international and internal structure of a nation does not necessarily change when it becomes independent: "The new nations preserve, above all, the dichotomous character and contradictory types of relations similar to those found in colonial society" (Horowitz, Castro, and Gerassi 1969, 130). Internal colonialism resembles the relations of domination and exploitation that are typical of the original colonialism.

Drawing upon the findings of anthropologists, he suggests that internal colonialism in Mexico assumes various forms. A dominant center or metropolis, such as the city of San Cristóbal, may hold a monopoly over Indian commerce and credit, resulting in monoculture (attention to a single crop), deformation, and dependence of the Indian economy.

Again, exploitation may be combined with feudalism, slavery, capitalism, forced and salaried work, and the like (Horowitz, Castro, and Gerassi 1969, 134). Thus internal colonialism is structural; it is tied to the policies of the national government and to the centers that perpetuate exploitation and dependence. The concept of internal colonialism helps to explain uneven development in underdeveloped countries, especially by encouraging examination of the laws of the market and the low level of political participation in underdeveloped areas, which "prevent the processes of egalitarianism characteristic of development from emerging."[32]

In a later work, González Casanova concentrates on the impact of imperialism on Latin America in the past and present,[33] and this work serves as the introduction to a two-volume study of country essays by distinguished Latin American scholars. For example, the essay on Brazil was written by Vania Bambirra and Theotonio dos Santos, two proponents of the theory of the new dependency, and the essay on Ecuador was prepared by Agustín Cueva, a critic of the idea of dependency from a classical Marxist viewpoint.[34]

González Casanova has also devoted considerable attention to concepts and methodology. In one study he set forth a research agenda, including suggested policies and planning for investigation in Mexico and Latin America, identification of social problems for study in the future, and a review of current research (see González Casanova and Bonfil 1968). He also identified the basic categories used by various specialists in economic development and discussed the ideological impact of capitalism and socialism on the use of these concepts (González Casanova 1967). As in his other writings, he attempted to find categories that would be applicable to investigation from either a capitalist or a socialist perspective. He suggested that four categories are applicable to the study of economic development: wealth, power, consciousness or values, and exploitation; the first three have been used since ancient times, the last by Marx. Kahl calls this "the most elegant of his writings, a tightly composed essay of just over 100 pages with a coherence derived from mature reflection" (Kahl 1976, 103; see 103–111 for an excellent summary). Finally, González Casanova devoted attention to the debate about scientific socialism and carefully examined Marxist terminology. He argued that many socialists have emphasized a democratic and nationalist project rather than looking at the important struggle between socialism and capitalism; thus they forget the importance of work, ownership of means of production, and relations of production. He also analyzed the transition to socialism and socialist hegemony, a process involving the working class and its access to power through contradictions of hegemony, autonomy, and representation (González Casanova 1982).

In summary, González Casanova has contributed to the theory of underdevelopment and development with his attention to such concepts as internal colonialism, exploitation, and imperialism. His work emphasizes a structural interpretation of society by identifying its dualistic character and examining the characteristics of backwardness in precapitalist and capitalist situations. González Casanova has assumed a socialist stance, but he believes that progressive capitalism must be permitted to embed itself in the marginal areas. Whether this situation is possible depends largely on the prospects for unity between the domestic or national bourgeoisie and the working class until the contradictions of capitalism and the development of working-class consciousness allow some movement in the direction of socialism. Mexico has contained much of the influence of imperialism, he argues, but internal colonialism remains an issue. He accepts the possibility of a violent revolution in the direction of socialism but believes that the Mexican system will evolve peacefully and with political and economic stability.

That view is evident in his assessment of the political reform of 1978 that expanded the possibilities of electoral participation in Mexico. For the parties on the left, he says, the reform signifies the need for a political pluralism; at the same time, the left must be careful not to be entrapped by liberalism, social democracy, or revolutionary nationalism. González Casanova remains optimistic: "For all the difficulties that the project of reform and democracy presents to groups that hold a socialist and social democratic perspective, it appears today as the only objectively viable alternative in which the Mexican people and its working class can live and struggle within the national and international context" (González Casanova 1979, 53).

Associated Dependent Capitalism: Fernando Henrique Cardoso

Fernando Henrique Cardoso was a professor at the University of São Paulo until his right to teach was revoked after the coup of 1964. Under the inspiration and supervision of the sociologist Florestán Fernandes, Cardoso worked with Octávio Ianni and others at the university on questions of slavery in the states of Paraná, Santa Catarina, and Rio Grande do Sul. The results were published in his doctoral thesis, published as *Capitalismo e escravidão* (1962).[35] Cardoso also published a study of the industrial entrepreneur and economic development in Brazil (Cardoso 1964).[36] In his early work, he acknowledged his preference for the dialectical method and the thought of Marx, but he also alluded to mainstream sociological writing and influential thinkers of his time such as Robert Merton, A. R. Radcliffe-Brown, Claude Lévi-Strauss, and others. From these writers, he drew the ideas of functionalism and structuralism that later were to permeate his own writings on dependency and underdevelopment. His approach to these problems took shape while Cardoso was in Santiago, Chile, at the Latin American Institute for Social and Economic Planning, an offshoot of ECLA, and the result was the publication with Enzo Faletto of *Dependencia y desarrollo en América Latina* (Cardoso and Faletto 1969, 1979).[37] During the seventies, Cardoso returned from exile to Brazil and settled in São Paulo where he headed the Centro Brasileiro de Análise e Planejamento (CEBRAP).[38]

Cardoso and Faletto see the ECLA paradigm for the analysis of development in Latin America as an alternative to the conservative emphasis on comparative advantages whereby some countries are seen as producers of raw materials and other countries are seen as producers of industrial goods.[39] Their approach is dialectical, emphasizing "not just the structural conditioning of social life, but also the historical transformation of structures by conflict, social movements, and class struggles" (Cardoso and Faletto 1979, x).[40] They also write about situations of dependency rather than about dependency theory and argue that rather than conceiving of dependency in a rather static way, the study of it must take into account forces of change and relate these forces to a global perspective. They stress a structural dependency that relates external and internal forces.

> We conceive the relationship between external and internal forces as forming a complex whole whose structural links are not based on mere external forms of exploitation and coercion, but are rooted in coincidence of interests between local dominant classes and international ones, and on the other side, are challenged by local dominated groups and classes. [Cardoso and Faletto 1979, xvi]

The external forces include multinational firms, foreign technology, international financial systems, foreign armies, and so on, which work on the behalf of imperialism. Domination of external forces may appear as an internal force through the practices of local classes and groups whose interests and values coincide with those of foreign ones.

Within this framework, Cardoso and Faletto are concerned with the degree to which industrialization and capital accumulation have advanced in the periphery. This periphery can only be understood in terms of the drive of advanced capitalist countries and their "incorporation of traditional noncapitalist economies into the world market."

Thus "the analysis of structural dependency aims to explain the interrelationships of classes and nation-states at the level of the international scene as well as at the level internal to each country" (Cardoso and Faletto 1979, xvii–xviii). Two basic situations of dependency are identified in their work: enclave economies, in which foreign investment penetrates into the local productive processes in the form of wages and taxes, and economies controlled by the local bourgeoisie, in which the starting point for the circulation of capital is internal, not external, and "accumulation is the result of the appropriation of natural resources by local entrepreneurs and the exploitation of the labor force by this same local group" (Cardoso and Faletto 1979, xix). They conclude that an economic system is dependent "when the accumulation and expansion of capital cannot find its essential dynamic component inside the system" (p. xx). Thus peripheral economies remain dependent even when they no longer produce only raw materials because their capital goods production cannot ensure their reproduction and expansion. These conditions characterize what is known as the "new dependency," in which industrialization in the periphery provides products not for mass consumption, as in the center, but for consumption by the bourgeoisie (Cardoso and Faletto 1979, xxi–xxii).

What, then, is the relationship of dependency to underdevelopment? For Cardoso and Faletto, underdevelopment evolves from the relations between peripheral and central societies. Societies experiencing underdevelopment have links with the world market, in the form of either peripheral colony or national state: "The situation of underdevelopment came about when commercial capitalism and then industrial capitalism expanded and linked to the world market non-industrial economies that went on to occupy different positions in the overall structure of the capitalist system" (Cardoso and Faletto 1979, 17).

Cardoso and Faletto reported that they did not view dependency and imperialism "as external and internal sides of a single coin" (Cardoso and Faletto 1979, xv).[41] Elsewhere, Cardoso had made his understanding of imperialism clearer. Having summarized Lenin's theory of imperialism, he suggested that although Lenin's insights were relevant to historical developments during the first half of the twentieth century, imperialism has entered a new stage since the Second World War and "the main points of Lenin's characterization of imperialism and capitalism are no longer fully adequate to describe and explain the present forms of capital accumulation and external expansion" (Cardoso 1972a, 87).

Mentioning the writings of Paul Baran and Paul Sweezy as works that explain the differences between capitalism in the present era and during the life of Lenin, Cardoso essentially accepted the premise that multinational and big corporate capital, rather than bank control and finance capital, now account for accumulation in the periphery. As a consequence of this accumulation, he said, new forms of economic dependency have appeared. For example, in countries like Brazil there is "an internal structural fragmentation connecting the most 'advanced' parts of their economies to the international capitalist system." In contrast to these advanced parts, the backward sectors of dependent countries act as "internal colonies," which produces a new type of dualism: "The new structural 'duality' corresponds to a kind of internal differentiation of the same unity" (Cardoso 1972a, 90).[42] Cardoso believed that imperialism in its present stage thus permits some local participation in economic production. That is, the big corporations allow a reorganization of the international division of labor so that some parts of dependent economies are included in their plans of productive investment. This tactic leads to internal fragmentation within these countries and sometimes to a shift in power; for example, the "modern" groups might replace the old oligarchical power groups. Cardoso argued that this interpretation was counter to the view of André Gunder Frank—for example, that imperialist capitalism promotes only underdevelopment in the periphery.

Cardoso elaborated on this position in some later essays. He called such development in the periphery "associated dependent development" and illustrated his model with evidence from the Brazilian experience. There, the power of the military regime that emerged after 1964 was shaped by new forms of national politics and new international economic forces. This "new bureaucratic-authoritarian political regime" was accompanied by "increased interdependence in production activities at the international level" and "a modification of the patterns of dependence that condition, or set constraints and limits to, the development of policies of the countries located at the periphery of the international capitalist system." Cardoso argued that "the dynamic basis of the production system [had] shifted" so that international capitalism predominated and industrial firms, whether owned by foreigners or nationals, were "linked to market, investment, and decisions located outside the country" (Cardoso 1973a, 146). Internally, the traditional agrarian landowners had lost much of their power base, and the domestic industrial and merchant interests found themselves in a disadvantageous position in relation to the new regime. The traditional and bureaucratic intermediate classes had lost prestige and influence.

Cardoso argued that these changes in power were attributable to the process of capital accumulation and the requirement that "the instruments of pressure and defense available to the popular classes be dismantled" (Cardoso 1973a, 147). The changes in the international capitalist system and, in particular, the impact of the multinational corporation allowed capital to penetrate into the peripheral economies so that "the interests of the foreign corporations become compatible with the internal prosperity of the dependent countries" and "promote development" (Cardoso 1973a, 149). Thus, as foreign capital directs itself toward the manufacturing and selling of products to be consumed by the domestic bourgeoisie, it can stimulate development in some segments of the economy of a dependent country: "Development under this set of conditions implies, quite obviously a definite articulation with the international market. . . . Development in this situation also depends on technological, financial, organizational, and market connections that only multinational corporations can assure" (Cardoso 1973a, 149).

This assumption led Cardoso to the conclusion that the 1964 coup had forced out the national bourgeoisie and statist developmental groups and replaced them with sectors of the international bourgeoisie. The economic policies and reforms that ensued were tied to international capitalism. Consequently, the Brazilian bourgeoisie could not carry out a bourgeois-democratic revolution; it could only tie itself to dependent capitalism by associating with international capital as a dependent and minor partner because capitalist accumulation in the periphery was unable to complete its cycle.

> Dependent capitalism must bear all the consequences of absorbing capital-intensive, labor-saving technology. . . . It is crippled because it lacks a fully developed capital goods sector. The accumulation, expansion, and self-realization of local capital requires and depends on a dynamic outside itself; it must insert itself into the circuit of international capitalism. [Cardoso 1973a, 163]

From this position, Cardoso attacked the speculation of Celso Furtado that the national bourgeoisie could contain international capitalism and promote development along autonomous and national lines. This approach, he believed, was no longer relevant because of the new hegemony under the military regime, and Furtado was overlooking the economic reality of associated dependent development.

Cardoso asserted not only that the dependent capitalist process of industrialization tends to occur under authoritarian regimes but that the dominant classes, in the face of internalization of production, must join with international capital and, at the same time, place demands on the state to implement policies that promote capitalist expansion. Controls over labor, expansion of state agencies, and establishment of public enterprise are ways in which an authoritarian regime promotes development policies in the image of the state. Such has been the experience of Brazil (Cardoso 1979b, 55).

Cardoso also has offered an appraisal of theories of dependency and underdevelopment. As a point of departure, he distinguished his own view—that the penetration of the periphery by industrial-financial capital accelerates the production of surplus value and intensifies the productive forces—from the view, espoused by such North American Marxists as Paul Baran, that capitalism leads to stagnation and underdevelopment in the periphery. He argued that the traditional currents in dependency thinking neither represented any new methodology nor contributed to intellectual history (Cardoso 1977b). Further, he criticized the analysis generated by dependency theorists for producing "images full of easy but misleading abstractions" around such terminology as development of underdevelopment, subimperialism, and revolution of marginals (Cardoso 1976, 1). He disputed the contention that capitalist development is impossible in the periphery, arguing that this emphasis on stagnation suggests leftist ideological inclinations. He contended with the development of underdevelopment thesis of André Gunder Frank and the more sophisticated assumptions of Ruy Mauro Marini. He also objected to the position of Frank and others that the local or national bourgeoisie is unable to accumulate capital. Likewise, he took exception to Marini's view that penetration by the multinational firm results in subimperialism or a policy of capitalist expansionism facilitated through the local state (Cardoso 1976, 3–15).

Elsewhere Cardoso identified the ideas of dependency in the classic works of Marx, Lenin, and Trotsky, claiming that they "used the expression with frequency." He considered the complaints of critics who characterized dependency theory as eclectic, schematic, petty-bourgeois, and so on, to be sterile and identified the efforts to develop a theory as ideological: "To the extent that 'dependency' has become a 'confused amalgam' of intermediate relations and articulations . . . and to the extent that it is an attempt to make a 'theory' out of the haziness of an obscure 'concept' then my immediate reaction is to refuse to give the label of science to this type of ideology" (Cardoso 1973b, 24).[43] This indictment is reiterated throughout Cardoso's work during the seventies: "If the ECLA theories are insufficient in characterization and in critique, the dependentistas, with all their love for a rational and integrated vision based on the experience of the European past, become surprisingly sterile: they proclaim what should not exist, but stop halfway to a concrete critique" (Cardoso 1979a, 28; see also 1980, 129–163).

The work of Cardoso has, of course, come under close scrutiny by critics. There are a few serious reviews of his works in English as well as a polemical attack by John Myer, who asserted that "the theory of Cardoso offers a non-revolutionary response as the preferred method of struggle in Brazil. . . . His claim that the theory of associated-dependent development is a guide to the struggle against imperialism is vacuous in the absence of an analysis of the extent to which finance capital is bank-rolling the development of the expanding state sector in Brazil" (Myer 1975, 47–48). Phillip O'Brien expressed concern that Cardoso's theory is simply an expression of bourgeois nationalism (O'Brien 1973). Robert Packingham (1982) has offered a more sympathetic appraisal.

Colin Henfrey, in a penetrating critique of the writings of Cardoso and Faletto, acknowledged their success in interpreting empirical data in historical analysis but felt that the complexity of their approach interfered with analysis of the present. The weakness of their work lies in "their theoreticization of the political in relation to the economic; an ensuing conceptual ambiguity, particularly regarding classes; and a consequently restricted focus of increasing significance through time . . . on ruling rather than the exploited classes" (Henfrey 1981, 29). Henfrey argued that unlike Frank and Marini, who respectively emphasize exchange and underconsumption in the sphere of circulation, Cardoso and Faletto locate their analysis in production and accumulation. At the same time, however, they emphasize the dominance of the political over the economic; that is, they see the ruling classes ruling through their power over other classes, not through economic mechanisms arising from their orientation to the international market. Thus Cardoso and Faletto are unable to offer a theory of the dominance of the political in the history of dependent social formations.

> Instead they tend merely to assume it empirically, with increasingly confused consequences. In effect, the internal becomes the political—as opposed to the primarily political expression of latently economic variables—and the external the economic; the priority of the political within the dependent social formation is no longer a function of the latter's specific economy and class relations but an assumed priority. In short, it ceases to be a Marxist and turns into a Weberian notion. From this theoretical ambiguity it is only a short conceptual step to seeing the political—as Cardoso and Faletto increasingly do—as a matter of relations between indeterminate groups and forces instead of between determinate classes. [Henfrey 1981, 30]

According to Henfrey, Cardoso and Faletto analyze on the level of group rather than class relations. Their conceptualization of class is inadequate and does not permit them to focus on the impact of dependency on exploited classes. This problem was also identified by Francisco Weffort in his criticism of Cardoso.

Among the Brazilian critics, Weffort warned that the concept of dependency runs the risk of being manipulated ideologically as well as serving as a substitute for such terms as "underdevelopment." He acknowledged two contributions in the work of the *dependentistas:* their critical appraisal of conventional theories of capitalist development and their focus on new theoretical questions. He distinguished two kinds of dependency in their work: external, involving the relations of peripheral nations with central nations, and structural, focusing on the impact of external relations on such internal structures as classes and relations of production. Cardoso and Faletto, he said, use this latter conception (Weffort 1971).

Weffort argued that dependency theory has served a purpose in criticizing the mechanical use of European and U.S. models in the interpretation of Latin America, but he concluded that "the criticism is incomplete on a theoretical level and insufficient on the political-ideological level" (Weffort 1971, 15). He considered dependency theory helpful in its assessment of dualism and the national bourgeoisie in Latin America and in its insistence on a global rather than a segmental perspective. However, he argued, the notion of structural dependency was drawn from the idea of nation and tied to the concept of class as if it were a theoretical principle. Weffort also believed that a theory of class does not necessitate emphasis on a national context in order to explain capitalist development and thus it ceases to be a theory altogether.

Cardoso responded to all this criticism by arguing that Weffort had "statically conceived an internal-external relationship and retraced an abstract dialectic of general and indeterminate contradictions" (Cardoso et al. 1971, 32). He insisted that a formal theory of classes cannot be substituted for a dialectical analysis of concrete situations of dependency. Classical theory, he repeated, is insufficient to analyze the new character of dependency.

This review suggests that although Cardoso and González Casanova undoubtedly advocate socialism for their societies, they also favor reformist policies and an evolutionary rather than a revolutionary approach to development. They refer to social classes but emphasize market and trade relations rather than relations of production, and thus they fail to employ a class analysis that examines conflict and struggle in depth. They look to the national bourgeoisie as a potential force for development. Their attention to these questions is not unrelated to concerns of Sunkel, Furtado, and Prebisch, who also look at the difficulties of capitalist reproduction in the periphery in contrast to the advances of the capitalist centers.

4 / Socialism and the Revolutionary Tradition

In contrast to the reformist traditions that evolved around the activities of ECLA, a parallel current of thought attempted to establish a scholarly basis for a revolutionry response to backwardness, exploitation, and underdevelopment. Three early figures of importance were Silvio Frondizi, Sergio Bagú, and Caio Prado Júnior. Later writers such as Theotonio dos Santos, Ruy Mauro Marini, and Aníbal Quijano elaborated on a revolutionary conception of underdevelopment. All participated in a socialist tradition.

Origins

Deformation in the Semicolony: Frondizi

Silvio Frondizi was born in 1907 in Paso de los Libres, Argentina. He earned degrees in history and law and taught at the University of Tucumán, the Colegio Libre de Estudios Superiores in Buenos Aires, and the University of Buenos Aires. With such books as *Introducción al pensamiento político de John Locke* (1944?), *La crisis política argentina* (1945), *El estado moderno* (1945), and his major work, *La realidad argentina* (1957), he established himself as one of Latin America's leading political scientists. Frondizi, a Marxist, opposed the intransigent policies of Argentine Communists and drew upon Trotsky's writings, especially *The Permanent Revolution* ([1930] 1962) and *History of the Russian Revolution* ([1932] 1959). He also founded a small revolutionary movement, the Movimiento Izquierda Revolucionario. In 1974, he was assassinated by right-wing terrorists.

Frondizi was concerned with questions of underdevelopment and dependency. The roots of this thinking first appear in an essay on world integration and capitalism (Frondizi 1947) in which he emphasized the contradictions in two imperialisms: British commercial imperialism and U.S. industrial imperialism. He also analyzed the links between imperialism and the national bourgeoisie in colonial and semicolonial countries. This work led to his criticism of the national bourgeoisie and to his attack on the thesis of a dual society that had been long advocated by the Communist parties of Latin America. Donald

Hodges (1974, 98–99) has suggested that Frondizi was thus the first to advocate the idea of a new dependency, which was to appear later in the writings of the Brazilian social scientist Theotonio dos Santos.

One of Frondizi's early associates, Marcos Kaplan, agreed that Frondizi was one of the first to express the idea of dependency and acknowledged that Trotskyist influence was evident in their movement, called Praxis. In particular, the Trotskyists Milcíades Peña and Nahuel Moreno (Hugo Bressano) pointed to the importance of British commercial imperialism and U.S. industrializing imperialism in Argentina. Within Praxis, Peña and Frondizi worked against the Stalinist line of the Argentine Communist party, and their ideas had much in common with Trotskyism, although, Kaplan insisted, Frondizi never was formally associated with the Fourth International.[44]

Frondizi's essay on world integration as the last stage of capitalism was written in the form of a response to the Argentine Communist leader Rodolfo Ghioldi, who had read an early version and offered a critique early in 1947.[45] Frondizi identified three periods in the evolution of the capitalist system. The first, studied by Marx, was that of national competition and was characterized by "a primary development of the capitalist system, based on free competition," and by "the social character of its production and the individual character of appropriation" (Frondizi 1947, 13–14). Frondizi argued that this form of capitalism could survive only with unlimited expansion of production. However, this capitalism was in fact limited not only by the level of productive forces and technology but by its own capitalist form. This contradiction resulted in a historical emphasis on nationalities. The second period, studied by Lenin, was represented by the formation of national imperialist systems and the substitution of monopolies for individual producers. The third period, in evidence after the Second World War, was dominated by world capitalist integration; Frondizi asserted that there had been a modification of the colonial situation rather than decolonization during this period. Whereas England during the colonial period had not experienced the rise of many national movements, in the current period the United States had assumed the leadership of the capitalist world and dominance over subjugated nations.

Frondizi's thinking was fully elaborated in his two-volume *La realidad argentina* (1957). In that work, he showed the inadequacy of the Argentine bourgeoisie, particularly within the movement around Juan Perón, to the task of realizing a bourgeois-democratic revolution. He attributed this inadequacy to conditions found in all semicolonial bourgeoisies because of their direct dependency on international monopoly capitalism (Frondizi 1957, 1:333). More generally, Frondizi was concerned with the struggle of a semicolonial nation to function during a period of industrial expansion elsewhere. He held that the large industrial centers, such as England, Germany, the United States, and Japan, were able to resolve their problems within the capitalist system along the lines of the bourgeois-democratic revolution, that is, through national independence, agrarian reform, industrial expansion, bourgeois democracy, and so on. The semicolonial and colonial nations of the periphery, which traditionally had provided raw materials, failed to benefit from the bourgeois-democratic revolution because of their economic and political dependence. The consequence for these nations was "a tremendous deforming impact, economically and politically" (Frondizi 1957, 1:27).

After a discussion of the evolution of capitalism along the lines of his 1947 essay, Frondizi examined the integrating force of the United States and its giant monopolies and imperialist endeavor and then went on to assess the degree of dependence or independence of national capital in the face of imperialism. He outlined the historical developments that had shaped Argentina's semicolonial character, including the impact of British capital on the agricultural and grazing sector, transportation, and industry. Whereas British capital directly financed domestic Argentine firms, U.S. capital was aimed at the establishment of subsidiaries of U.S. firms in Argentina. Given these conditions, the Peronistas had attempted to defend the national bourgeoisie in the face of imperialism, but the disintegration of this bourgeoisie had simply led to the strengthening of the state apparatus itself and eventually to the increased dominance of imperialism. Thus the process of industrialization in an underdeveloped country represented a tendency toward greater, rather than lesser, dependency on the advanced centers of the world; industrial development was accompanied by increased imperialist domination through the establishment of branch firms and the integration of the domestic market and the national bourgeoisie into the international economy under the control of monopoly capital.

In summary, basing his ideas on the thought of Marx, Lenin, and Trotsky, Frondizi elaborated a theory of the relationship of dependent, peripheral, and underdeveloped nations to dominant, central, and advanced ones. He showed how monopoly capital and imperialism cause the disintegration of national capital. He argued that in the era of industrial capitalism a national bourgeoisie could not succeed in promoting autonomous capitalism. Thus intervention by the state, subsidization, and reformist policies were useless. The only solution lay in the path to socialism. Frondizi outlined in considerable detail how this path could be followed: He identified the conditions allowing for revolution, the seizure of power by the proletariat, and the establishment of the transition to socialism (Frondizi 1957, vol. 2). Like many of his contemporaries he focused on the Cuban Revolution as an example (Frondizi 1960).

Capitalism and Class Struggle: Bagú

The historian Sergio Bagú is often cited in the literature on underdevelopment for having set forth important ideas about the relationship of the advanced capitalist nations to backward colonial areas. Bagú is best remembered for his research and writing on the colonial period in Latin America in general and in Argentina in particular. Born and educated in Argentina, he taught for a number of years at the University of Buenos Aires. Among his works on colonialism are *Vida de José Ingenieros* (1936), *Vida de Mariano Moreno* (1939), *Economía de la sociedad colonial* (1949), *Estructura social de la colonia* (1952), and *El plan económico del grupo rivadaviano (1811-1827)* (1966).

His interpretation of colonial history was developed in lectures in the United States from 1944 to 1946 and is contained in his 1949 book on the economic structure of the colonial regimes in Spanish and Portuguese Latin America. The first part of this work looks at pre-Columbian economy; the second, at the colonial economy; and the third, at the world economic struggle and the process of production on the margin of colonial society (Bagú 1949).

The thesis of this work is that capitalism made its impact on Latin America very early. Bagú confirmed the observation of several writers that at the beginning of the sixteenth century, Portugal was no longer feudal. King Manuel I, with his policies of navigation and discovery, his control of commerce outside Portugal, and his regime of international monopolies, was "an authentic capitalist" (Bagú 1949, 54). Although Portuguese merchant capital ensured control over Brazil and other foreign areas, it was not used to break feudal conditions of production at home, and therefore the national economy proceeded at its medieval pace.

Bagú emphasized that Europe dominated the international markets and shaped the structure of the colonial economies. These economies were subordinated to the foreign market—"the principal factor of deformation and stagnation." Later, he argued, the political economy of the European metropolises would "accentuate the economic dependency of the colonies, but the appearance of a larger internal colonial market in the Spanish regions would make the conditions of dependency there greater than in the Portuguese regions" (Bagú 1949, 68).

He went on to show that the present economies of Latin America preserve many of the fundamental characteristics of these colonial structures. He described the dominance of the Iberian monarchies as being like "a giant feudal enterprise" (Bagú 1949, 98), yet incorporating early capitalism. He labeled such institutions as the *encomienda* and *donatarios* (entrustments or grants of Indians and land grants) as feudal, but he considered that they were limited in their influence upon Latin America. The feudal cycle was not particularly strong in the Iberian Peninsula, and it did not reproduce itself in the colonies. Instead, the colonies were integrated into a new capitalist cycle (Bagú 1949, 103).

Bagú analyzed the elements of the capitalist configuration in colonial Latin America, emphasizing the accumulation of capital, financial capital, production for market, and commerce. In discussing the relationship of city and countryside, he reaffirmed that the "economic regime of the colonial period was not feudalism but colonial capitalism. . . . Far from reviving a feudal cycle, America entered a cycle of commercial capitalism, already inaugurated in Europe, with surprising speed" (Bagú 1949, 143). Spain and Portugal, he argued, had never been as feudal as other European countries, because of the Arab invasion of the Iberian Peninsula and the struggle for reconquest that had followed. "The war, by imposing a military discipline . . . had weakened feudalism and put in the hands of the kingdom a unification and power that proved decisive in the latter period of the peninsular Middle Ages" (Bagú 1949, 31–32). Furthermore, Spain and Portugal had experienced merchant capital since the thirteenth century, and Barcelona had benefited from the intense commerce in the Mediterranean under the control of "a rich bourgeoisie of traders who defended their interests against feudal remnants and the absorbing tendency of the Catalan-Aragon monarchy" (Bagú 1949, 35). There also was a financial organization in the hands of private capitalists that backed the monarchical-military enterprise and bolstered the large armies of the peninsula. Bagú argued that merchant and financial capital were thus combined during this period, although merchant capital was "the motor force of the overseas adventures" (Bagú 1949, 41).

Bagú systematically examined the accumulation of capital in the colonies, arguing that the considerable quantities of money in circulation during the sixteenth century in Latin America demonstrated that the economy could not have been feudal. He identified merchant capital in the mines of Mexico as early as the middle of the century, commercial firms in Peru during the seventeenth century, the cacao plantations of Venezuela, and the black slave traffic. He showed that finance capital was in evidence as early as the sixteenth century as miners, merchants, large farmers, and slave traders made use of credit, loaning money to small merchants and farmers. Thus it was not feudalism but colonial capitalism that appeared in Latin America during this period (Bagú 1949, 113–114).

In later works, Bagú turned to contemporary developments and focused on social classes, cultural development, and the relationship between the nation and the international situation. For example, his clearest and most definitive treatment of social classes in Latin America offered both conceptualization and historical interpretation (Bagú 1952). Using the framework of his earlier economic analysis of colonial society, Bagú traced the origins and evaluations of social classes and relations of production. He examined the role of the Hispanic-Portuguese colonial experience and such conditional elements as ethnic groups and the church in the formation of social classes. He looked at class conflict and violence in the face of the colonial political and juridical order.

One of his better-known works is his *Argentina en el mundo* (1960), which offers an interpretive overview of Argentina in the world setting, with attention to the nineteenth and twentieth centuries. His historical treatment is less theoretical and less political in orientation and more concerned with the organization and analysis of factual material. He discussed the relationship between the national state and its international orientation and insisted that rather than envisioning the nation as a homogeneous entity whose interests are based on conduct abroad, the nation should be seen as a heterogeneous whole, dependent on its internal structures but searching for a solution to national needs in the extranational arena.

In another work, Bagú examined the theme of cultural development in the liberation of Latin America, addressing issues in a somewhat abstract manner. Technology, he argued, is an instrument "that can exterminate peoples." Culture, in contrast, stimulates the formation of personality, although under the control of cultural elements, "mediocre and totally subordinated personalities" are subject to "a spiritual slavery" (Bagú et al. 1967, 11–12). He wrote about the international division of cultural work and the control of culture under capitalist and socialist societies, concentrating on historical example rather than on a theoretical framework to illustrate his analysis.

Bagú also was interested in social stratification. In a brief account of social stratification in Argentina, he presented historical data on the economy, examined social stratification and national structure, and specifically looked at consumption, knowledge, and power as elements that must be understood in a class analysis (Bagú 1969). In a later essay, he returned to the ideas in his earlier work on colonialism and discussed Latin American society in terms of a system of stratification involving the popular masses, old and new dominant classes, and intermediate strata. He related metropoles to world capitalism in his focus on dependent capitalism. He emphasized the domination of international capital and argued that dependency may increase as the industrial sector grows and modernizes. He focused on the overlapping of such terms as "decadence," "underdevelopment," "development," and "dependency" in study of social classes in situations of underdevelopment in Latin America (Bagú et al. 1975).

Capitalism, Not Feudalism: Prado

Caio Prado Júnior was born in 1907 and established himself in São Paulo as author, historian, social critic, politician, founder and head of a publishing house, and the editor of the Marxist social science journal, *Revista Brasiliense*. He was also a member of the Brazilian Communist party, and after the Second World War, he served that party as an elected representative to the Brazilian Congress. He frequently disagreed, however, with the intransigent party position, particularly on feudalism, which he claimed had had no influence on Brazil. Prado's major work, like that of Bagú, focused on the colonial formation of Brazil. The essence of his thought is found in several volumes on this theme, the most important being *The Colonial Background of Modern Brazil* (1967).[46]

Prado believed that the discovery and colonization of the Americas was an episode in the history of European maritime expansion after the fifteenth century as colonization implied the establishment of trading stations and commercial enterprise: "Colonization of the tropics appears as one vast commercial enterprise, more complex than the old trading stations but retaining the flavor of these, the foremost objective being the exploitation of the natural resources of a virgin land for the benefit of European commerce" (Prado Júnior 1967, 20). Prado elaborated on this generalization with a detailed historical analysis of the evolution of the Brazilian economy. His analysis can be outlined in the form of a number of propositions.

First, three sectors composed the economy of colonial Brazil. There was the agrarian organization, consisting of the large estate, slave labor, and monoculture. The ownership of the large estate involved large-scale exploitation of it and, together with monoculture and slave labor, formed a large-scale rural enterprise, that is, "a large number of individuals brought together to form a *single unit of production*, which became the basic cell of the Brazilian agrarian economy . . . the principal base on which the whole economic and social structure of the country was founded" (Prado Júnior 1967, 138). There was also mining, which was characterized by activities and organization similar to those of the agrarian sector: "It was thus exploitation on a large scale that prevailed: large units worked by slaves" (Prado Júnior 1967, 139). Finally, there was the extractive sector, concentrated in the Amazon Valley where cacao, nuts, and other forest products were collected. Prado again pointed to the prevalence of large units of production:

> It was still a large productive unit insofar as it brought together a relatively large number of workers under the orders and on the behalf of a single entrepreneur. . . . It is in this system of organizing labor and property that lies the origin of the extreme concentration of wealth that characterized the colonial economy. [Prado Júnior 1967, 140]

Prado summed up the basic characteristics of the Brazilian economy as related, on the one hand, to this organization of production and labor and the concentration of wealth that was generated from this organization and, on the other hand, to an externally oriented economy based on production of commodities for the international market.

Second, this orientation to the international market was a reflection of policies of Portugal that aimed at enriching that country through trade. Independent commercial activities by Brazilian traders were suppressed. Efforts to set up manufacturing industries failed, and Brazil was reduced to the status of a producer of certain commodities for international trade.

Third, the Brazilian economy was characterized by a cyclical pattern of prosperity and decline. Initially, the sugar-producing areas of Bahia and Pernambuco were affected by such cyclical development, at first prospering because of worldwide demand and later declining in the face of international competition and abundant supplies. The rise and decline of sugar was followed by a similar pattern in mining and cotton. Prado suggested that this pattern was merely a reflection of the precarious foundations of the Brazilian economy, which was designed for external consumption and had no autonomous existence: "It did not create the foundation needed to support and maintain a population dependent on such a structure: an organized system of production and distribution of resources for the material subsistence of the population" (Prado Júnior 1967, 145). Stagnancy and reliance on international trade thus were the results of three centuries of rise and decline.

Fourth, Brazilian industry was in only a rudimentary stage as late as the beginning of the nineteenth century, the consequence of Portuguese colonial policy and the economic system itself: "If the country's political and administrative situation, as a mere colonial appendage of a shortsighted mother country that was jealous of its privileges, was a serious handicap to its industrial development, the economic regime was even more to blame" (Prado Júnior 1967, 263). This period's rather primitive manufacturing activities described by Prado could not be compared to what is today understood as industrialization.

Fifth, Portugal was simply an intermediary between the colonial sources of supply of tropical products and the European markets. Prado demonstrated that although Portugal appeared as a power among European nations, some two-thirds of its exports to other countries consisted of colonial products. This condition placed Portugal in a weakened position so that once Brazil broke free in the nineteenth century, "Portugal, once a great power, passed from the middling power she had become to the mediocrity of one of Europe's most insignificant countries" (Prado Júnior 1967, 275).

Sixth, commerce was prominent, allowing the merchants "to make a stand against the colony's other proprietary class, the landowners, and dispute their preeminence." Prado suggested that a class struggle between these groups ensued: "There was a repetition in Brazil of the traditional rivalry between noblemen and bourgeoisie which fills the history of Europe." This struggle was sharpened by nationalist loyalties, the merchants favoring Portugal, where most had been born, and the planters, descendants of the pioneer settlers, supporting Brazil. Prado showed how this rivalry manifested itself in a series of violent outbreaks that both preceded and followed independence (Prado Júnior 1967, 344–346).

Prado's analysis clearly moves in a socialist direction. During the early sixties, he published a work that he described simply as impressions of the travels of a communist to socialist countries (Prado Júnior 1962). This work distinguishes between capitalism and socialism. Capitalism, even "reformist" capitalism, will be eliminated through its own contradictions: "Capitalism essentially signifies antagonism, struggle. Human relations, within the system, are always established at the base on conflict of interests." Socialism evolves from capitalism: "It is a natural result of capitalism." Socialism, he believed, involves cooperation among men, a common force that carries all toward the same end. Whereas capitalism emphasizes particular and individual interests, socialism builds on a base of general interests. The evolution from capitalism to socialism implies the abolition of free economic initiative and of the dominance of the private sector over the forces of production. No other alternative is available to the contemporary world. "What constitutes the essence of socialism is the substitution of free economy, characteristic of capitalism and the antagonism among individuals . . . by the coordination of economic action in the interest of the collective society" (Prado Júnior 1962, 5, 8, 19, 26–27). He went on to discuss the implications of freedom in capitalist and socialist societies, the state under socialism and the dictatorship of the proletariat, the role of the Communist party, and the march toward communism. He condemned any advocacy of simplistic solutions; he understood socialism not as dogma or arbitrary norm or recipe but as part of a process involving the breakdown of capitalism.

Prado was concerned with Brazilian nationalism and the struggle to confront foreign capital. As political thought, nationalism reflected the consciousness of Brazilians of the "dependent and subordinate situation the country faces in relation to the large financial and capitalist centers of the contemporary world." Such a situation, he asserted, was typical of "a peripheral country in the capitalist system . . . a country situated on the margin of that system and complementary to it." Thus the material level of Brazil remained lower than that of most capitalist nations (Prado Júnior 1955, 82). Brazilian industrialization, subject to the initiative of international firms, was, he argued, limited by an export economy "of primary products oriented to the consumption by dominant areas in the international system of capitalism, in which we continue our traditional peripheral and dependent position" (Prado Júnior 1959, 14). A nationalist policy, he believed, could give impetus to economic development and raise the standard of living by assuming control over the forces of production that were subsidiary to international commerce.

During the early sixties, nationalism was evident among political parties, labor unions, peasant leagues, and other groups that agitated for reform and change in Brazil. The military intervention in 1964, however, brought an abrupt halt to these activities and was accompanied by political repression. Prado reassessed his position and, in a controversial book on the Brazilian "revolution," set forth his views.

Socialism, he argued, would be the consequence of the Brazilian revolution: "Socialism is the direction in which capitalism marches. It is the dynamic of a capitalism projected into its future" (Prado Júnior 1966, 10). Although critical of the dogmatism and sectarianism that had characterized communist thinking in the past (which he attributed primarily to Stalinism), he argued that Marxism, with its dialectical method, offered the possibility of a new historical interpretation and analysis.

The Marxist theory of the Brazilian revolution, he pointed out, can be traced to the decade of the twenties when colonial, semicolonial, and dependent countries were politically and economically submissive to imperialism. At the time it was assumed that these countries were not experiencing any appreciable development. Further, it was believed, it conformity with Lenin's thinking about czarist Russia, that a bourgeois-democratic revolution would allow for the transition from remnants of feudalism to capitalism. Such a revolution took an anti-imperialist and agrarian direction—anti-imperialist in opposition to the domination of the capitalist powers and agrarian in the struggle against feudalism. In this scheme, the colonial and semicolonial nations of Asia were lumped together with the dependent nations of Latin America. According to Prado, this model was irrelevant to the experience of Brazil because feudalism had never existed there (Prado Júnior 1966, 51).[47] On the basis of this position, he attacked the programs of the Brazilian Communist party, especially those of 1954 ("deformed with serious errors of interpretation of the Brazilian reality") and 1960 ("reflected a contradiction between theory and practical experience") (Prado Júnior 1966, 80–81).

Prado showed that in Asian countries, especially China, the bourgeoisie, composed of merchants, especially those tied to the import and export of international products, was pro-imperialist. Any national bourgeoisie in Brazil would be led by industrialists opposed to imperialism and the exploitation of Brazilian resources. The appearance in Brazil of international trusts and monopolies, however, undermined any effort to establish domestic industry. Even the most progressive of Brazilian industrialists began to associate with these foreign firms by establishing ties with international economic and financial interests. Thus, Prado said, what is commonly understood as a progressive national bourgeoisie was not evident in Brazil. Illusions about a progressive national bourgeoisie had resulted in the disaster of April 1964, for the Brazilian left had developed the false conviction that the pseudonational bourgeois sectors were leading an anti-imperialist and antifeudal struggle.

Given that feudalism was not an issue and a national bourgeoisie could not lead the reformist effort to confront imperialism in Brazil, Prado concluded that only a revolutionary course remained. Because imperialism had deep roots in Brazil, economic dependence and submission to imperialism would have to be broken by revolutionary struggle and national liberation. The periphery would have to break with imperialism and the international system of capitalism. The struggle in Brazil would be similar to that of revolutionary nations in Africa and Asia, and there would have to be elimination of the economic and social elements that constituted the internal colonial formation (Prado Júnior 1966, 308).

In summary, Frondizi, Bagú, and Prado sought socialism as a solution to the underdevelopment and dependency that had shaped the periphery since colonial times. They analyzed the problems of the periphery in terms of capitalism as contrasted with feudalism and attempted to show the negative consequences of imperialism and the international system of capitalism. They attributed the deformation of the periphery to its dependency on monopoly capital and the impact of foreign firms on domestic economies. All three based their analysis on Marx—Frondizi was influenced also by Trotsky; Prado, by Lenin. All three used class analysis, distinguishing ruling classes from working class and subsistence mass. They questioned the idea of a dual society, since they did not consider feudalism a major mode of production. They were suspicious of interpretations that emphasized the progressive role of a national bourgeoisie in the face of international capital. They rejected the bourgeois-democratic revolution as a solution to the crisis of capitalism in the Third World.

New Directions

The New Dependency: Dos Santos

Theotonio dos Santos formulated his thinking on underdevelopment and dependency during the years of nationalism and political mobilization in Brazil. He was associated with the University of Brasília in the early sixties, and after the 1964 coup, he became affiliated with the Centro de Estudios Socioeconómicos of the University of Chile. With his wife, Vania Bambirra,[48] he brought together a number of Chilean and Brazilian social scientists, including Ruy Mauro Marini, to study imperialism and its impact on dependent societies. The Chilean coup of 1973 forced him to seek refuge in Mexico where he continued his research and writing at the Universidad Nacional Autónoma de México.

In a seminal piece published in English, Dos Santos offered a conceptualization of dependency:

> By dependence we mean a situation in which the economy of certain countries is conditioned by the development and expansion of another economy to which the former is subjected. The relation of interdependence between two or more economies, and between these and world trade, assumes the form of dependence when some countries (the dominant ones) can expand and can be self-sustaining, while other countries (the dependent ones) can do this only as a reflection of that expansion, which can have either a positive or negative effect on their immediate development. [Dos Santos 1970d, 231][49]

This widely accepted conception of dependency focuses on the relationship of two countries, especially when dependency results in the expansion of dominant countries. Dos Santos accepted the Marxist theory of the expansion of imperialist centers and their domination over the world economy but also saw a need for a theory that addressed the laws of internal development in those countries that are the object of such expansion. He hoped to move beyond contemporary theories of development and modernization that stress capitalism in the image of the advanced countries as a means to overcome backwardness. Instead, he emphasized the unequal and combined nature of development, concepts evident in Trotskyist writing. Apparently influenced also by Paul Baran, Dos Santos held that unequal trade relations based on monopolistic control at the center result in transfers of surplus from dependent to dominant countries. Such inequality produces limits within the dependent countries on the capacity of the internal market as well as negative consequences for the people: "We call this combined development because it is the combination of these inequalities and the transfer of resources from the most backward and dependent sectors to the most advanced and dominant ones which explains the inequality, deepens it, and transforms it into a necessary and structural element of the world economy" (Dos Santos 1970d, 231).[50]

Dos Santos distinguished three historical forms of dependency. First, there was colonial dependency in which trade monopolies were established over the land, mines, and labor of colonial societies. Second, financial-industrial dependency acompanied the period of imperialism at the end of the nineteenth century and allowed the domination of big capital in the hegemonic centers and its expansion abroad. Finally, a new type of dependency appeared in the era after the Second World War, this period being characterized by capital investment of multinational corporations in industry oriented to the internal markets of underdeveloped countries.

Analyzing the relations of dependency, Dos Santos showed that the possibility for investment in a country depends on the availability of financial resources for the purchase of machinery and raw materials not available domestically. These financial resources are usually dependent on the export sector for foreign exchange, which is conditioned by fluctuations in the balance of payments. He also looked at the effect of these international relations on productivity. First, the need to preserve the structure of agrarian and mining exports affects relations between the advanced centers that export surplus value from the backward areas as well as between the internal dominant metropolitan centers and the dependent colonial areas; the unequal and combined capitalist development on the international level is reproduced on the internal national level. Second, the structure of industry and technology relates to the interests of the multinational corporations rather than to the needs of the population and national capital interests of a dependent country. The consequences of these relations are high concentration of income, exploitation of labor power, and adoption of a technology of intensive capital use: "The alleged backwardness of these economies is not due to a lack of integration with capitalism but . . . on the contrary, the most powerful obstacles to their full development come from the way in which they are joined to this international system and its laws of development" (Dos Santos 1970d, 235).

Dos Santos concluded that the system of dependent reproduction is part of a system of world economic relations based on monopolistic control of capital. A system of dependent production and reproduction leads to backwardness and misery, and whatever capitalist development is produced by this system tends to benefit only a small segment of a population. This situation results in serious structural problems, which, in turn, lead to more dependency and superexploitation.

The solution to the problem he offered was a revolutionary one. He felt that the developmentalist path suggested by ECLA and other international agencies could not destroy "these terrible chains imposed by dependent development" (Dos Santos 1970d, 236).[51] The best hope, he said, rested in a confrontation between military regimes and fascism, on the one hand, and popular revolutionary governments and socialism, on the other—"intermediate solutions have proved to be, in such a contradictory reality, empty and utopian" (Dos Santos 1970d, 236). He went on to review the prospects for such a solution.

During the sixties, Latin America had seen the emergence of a popular movement composed of sectors of the industrial bourgeoisie and the petty bourgeoisie that favored autonomous national development as an alternative to traditional efforts to solve the dilemma of under-development. This movement had organized itself—politically, ideo-logically, and strategically—in a radical direction, often embracing the idea of establishing a socialist society. Various political currents had evolved, some favoring electoral tactics and pressure upon a populist government and others supporting popular insurrection, first in the countryside and then in the city. As the former failed to transform societies through peaceful means, the latter began to have an impact. These different groups were particularly influenced by the example of the Cuban Revolution, but they also counted on the radicalized sectors of the nationalist element. Emphasis on insurrection shifted after the death in Bolivia of Ché Guevara to the idea of armed struggle and popular war.

Dos Santos believed that this new movement offered considerable hope for solving the problems of underdevelopment in Latin America. He felt that the model of popular revolutionary war was appropriate to the particular historical circumstances: the failure of the nationalist path and the impact of the multinationals on the interior of each country; the inability of the national system to respond to the contradictions generated by dependent capitalist development; the formation of an independent popular movement under bourgeois leadership; the coalition of this leadership with radical elements in the confrontation with the institutional violence of the dominant classes; and the legitimization of this coalition and its tendency to expand its struggle to the continental level. Dos Santos also outlined a revolutionary strategy involving a revolutionary war on a continental scale that would progressively unify mass forces and establish political-military organizations to lead the struggle through well-organized, armed, ideological fronts. He saw obstacles to this struggle in a tendency of the Latin American left to follow mechanically in the path of other revolutionaries rather than to formulate a theory based on its own experience, its inclination to disperse into undisciplined ideological groupings, and its habit of initiating political actions that ignored the level of political development of the masses (Dos Santos 1970b).

In a more recent work, Dos Santos examined the theory of development and identified the crisis of its model, then elaborated on the concept of dependency and its theoretical antecedents in Marx, and Lenin, and other writers. He reaffirmed his own position concerning the new dependency and analyzed the prospects for socialism in terms of the historical experience of contemporary Latin America (Dos Santos 1978, 281–470).

Subimperialism: Ruy Mauro Marini

The economist Ruy Mauro Marini was prominent in Brazilian politics during the early sixties. As an activist and intellectual, he was a product of the leftist movements of the time that linked nationalism with Marxism. After the coup of 1964 he fled into exile in Chile, where he began to develop his thinking on dependency in association with the Centro de Estudios Socioeconómicos. As a consequence of the Chilean coup of September 1973, Marini moved to Mexico, where he became associated with the Centro de Información, Documentación y Análisis sobre el Movimiento Obrero Latinoamericano. He is the author of several popular books and a number of significant articles. Calling for revolutionary action, Marini aligned himself politically with the thesis of Frank and others that capitalism creates deformation and underdevelopment in the periphery; economically, however, he focused on production rather than, as Frank did, on circulation. Dependent capitalism, Marini believed, is unable to reproduce itself through the process of accumulation. Under such conditions, absolute surplus value can be realized in the periphery, through lengthening the workday and intensifying the use of labor power, but relative surplus value, derived by lowering the cost of labor through technology and an increase in productivity, cannot. Because the consumption of workers is insignificant and the economy tends to be based on the export of raw materials and other products, the prospects for industrialization are not great. Thus a dependent capitalist economy tends to expand by pushing beyond its national borders and dominating the economies of weaker neighbors. This process is called subimperialism (Marini 1973a, 1973b).

According to Marini, the Second World War resulted in a period of crisis and the rise of new tendencies in the accumulation of capital. In particular, the United States reorganized the world capitalist economy to ensure the distribution of a large commercial surplus generated by high productivity at home and to extend its sphere of influence to areas of the periphery. This reorganization was accomplished through the formation of the World Bank and the International Monetary Fund as well as other trade and financial treaties and agreements that allowed U.S. domination over the international economy. With the expansion of world capitalism, private capital flowed into Latin America. In one dependent country, Brazil, the military took control, reordered the economy and the structure of the class forces, repressed the working class and opposition, and launched a "project" of subimperialism. "Brazilian subimperialism is not only the expression of an economic phenomenon. It results from the process of class struggle in the country and from the political project defined by the technocratic military team which assumed power in 1964, combined with the conjunctural conditions in the world economy and in world politics" (Marini 1978b, 34). More specifically, subimperialism has two components, one relating to national policy regarding productivity and the work force and the other to an autonomous expansionist policy: "on the one hand, a medium organic composition on the world scale of national productive apparatus, and, on the other, the exercise of a relatively autonomous expansionist policy which is not only accompanied by a greater integration in the imperialist productive system but also is maintained under the hegemony exercised by imperialism on an international scale" (Marini 1978b, 34–35).

Marini related these ideas to Brazil, where the military dictatorship had been established, in his view, as a consequence of capitalist development and "a desperate attempt to open it to new perspectives of development" (Marini 1969, 111). The dictatorship moved to intervene in the unions and other organizations of the working class and jailed and assassinated labor and peasant leaders. Given this offensive against the popular forces, the military also had to reinforce a coalition of the ruling classes by reestablishing the compromise between the bourgeoisie and the landowner-merchant oligarchy. The government facilitated investment and the introduction of new technology, thus intensifying capitalization of the countryside. At the same time, it provided incentives for foreign investment. The consequence of this integration with imperialism was not only an increase in industrial productive capacity but also a disruption of the labor force. The principal problem was the inability of Brazilian industrial capitalism to create new domestic markets that could absorb the increasing productivity. This contradiction could be resolved, if only partially, through an expansion into new markets, especially in Latin America.

Thus Brazilian subimperialism ultimately depended on the capital and technology of the North American monopolies, and Brazilian capitalism had reached the stage of imperialism without effecting any overall change in the national economy and its increasing dependence on international capitalism (Marini 1969, 115). Under these conditions, Brazilian subimperialism could not utilize exploitation of neighboring countries as a means of raising the standard of living within the country. Thus an autonomous capitalist development could not occur in Brazil, nor could a national bourgeoisie play any significant role in Brazilian development.

Given this situation, the mass of workers would lead Brazil along a revolutionary course. Solidarity among the exploited classes and the emergence of a vast political movement would allow the proletariat to sharpen the contradiction between the bourgeoisie and the landowner-merchant oligarchy, impede foreign investment, and promote autonomous development. Marini concluded that compromises and reforms could not lead to a solution and that the working class must resort to the revolutionary struggle against the subimperialist bourgeoisie and imperialism itself (Marini 1969, 119–120). Armed struggle would characterize the revolution of the masses and a vanguard of the petty bourgeoisie. The role of this vanguard would be, not to lead this movement, but to fight alongside the workers (Marini 1969, 160–162).

In summary, Marini offered a framework in which underdevelopment was a consequence of dependent capitalism in Latin America.[52] He based his framework on passages in Marx referring to dominant and subordinate relations of development and lack of development (Marini 1973b, 15–16, 83). He held that Frank's development-of-underdevelopment thesis led to "impeccable" political conclusions but criticized its assumption that a colonial situation was similar to a dependency situation (Marini 1973b, 18–19). Marini set forth what he called a Marxist theory of dependency, but he also insisted that capitalist development could accompany economic dependency. He offered the idea of subimperialism to help explain how such development takes place within a dependent economy and to highlight one of its consequences, the exploitation of labor. Inevitably, a revolutionary, not a reformist, course would be required to overcome this exploitation.[53]

The Marini thesis was systematically criticized by José Serra and Fernando Henrique Cardoso (Serra and Cardoso 1978). Marini, in response, offered a detailed rejoinder (1978a). Fundamentally, their differences, as summarized by Henfrey, are as follows: Marini emphasized laws of dependent capitalism whereas Cardoso favored concrete situations of dependence; Marini attacked Cardoso as a defender of the bourgeoisie, whereas Cardoso condemned Marini's advocacy of armed struggle as voluntarist and ineffective. Henfrey considered Cardoso the winner of this debate: The armed struggle favored by Marini had failed in Brazil, and his problematic "blocks any concrete analysis of class struggle" (Henfrey 1981, 23–24). Henfrey criticized Marini for his economism or economic determinism: "In part then the issue at stake is one which lies at the heart of Marxist thinking: the relations between base and superstructure and the very nature of class itself, as more or less economically determined. . . . Yet Marini's position is distinct even within the contentious premise of such economic determinism" (Henfrey 1981, 24). Henfrey objected that Marini had not only characterized the laws of motion as economically determined but located them in dependent capitalism: "This conflation in 'dependent capitalism' of two concepts of such different status as mode of production and social formation . . . is intrinsically anti-analytic." Henfrey was equally critical of Cardoso, especially his "theoretical vagueness." For Henfrey, the debate served to expose the weaknesses of dependency formulations.

> As shown by Cardoso's debate with Marini, the alternative search
> for a generalized model and autonomous theory of dependence—at
> heart an ideological one—appropriated the terms of discussion,
> stunting the much more methodological, concrete, and analytic option.
> Hence the striking features of dependency writing as typified in
> this debate are its overemphasis on the external, its economism at
> the expense of an understanding of the social relations of production,
> and its repetitive generality, with the lasting dearth of substantive
> case studies. [Henfrey 1981, 27]

Dependency, Imperialism, and the
Class Struggle: Aníbal Quijano

The Peruvian political sociologist Aníbal Quijano has had a substantial impact upon students of Latin America. As a scholar and an intellectual, his writing has contributed to an understanding of contemporary Peru. He has first and foremost been concerned with an analysis of imperialism and its consequences for the domestic political economy, which has led him to an examination of class forces and struggle in Peru. Second, Quijano has engaged intellectually with prevailing interpretations of his society and has assumed an activist political role in an effort to shape its direction and destiny along a socialist path.[54] In this role, he has launched a quarterly publication, *Sociedad y Política*, which is respected for its insights and criticism.

In *Nationalism and Capitalism in Peru: A Study in Neo-Imperialism* (1971), he offered a tentative examination of the economic policies of the military junta that governed Peru from October 1968 until early 1971. Part of the book had circulated in preliminary form at the University of Chile, where Theotonio dos Santos, Vania Bambirra, and Ruy Mauro Marini were studying imperialism and dependency. Quijano's analytical framework was based on a conception of dependency and a focus on social classes and their relations outside Peru. His analysis of the military regime suggested that a small nationalist bourgeoisie was unlikely to be able to overcome imperialist domination.

He saw two kinds of imperialism operating in Peru and Latin America in general: traditional imperialism, with the United States as the hegemonic power through agro-extractive enterprises controlled by foreign capital, and a more recent imperialism, evident since the Second World War, brought about by manufacturing in urban areas. White-collar workers and the petty bourgeoisie had begun to assert demands, and the industrial proletariat was expanding; at the same time, peasant movements had appeared in the countryside. Threatened by pressures for popular revolution, the power base of the new bourgeoisie had fragmented, necessitating the intervention and seizure of control by the armed forces. After coming to power, the military regime had attempted to eliminate foreign control of production in agricultural exports, mining, and petroleum and, at the same time, had also attempted to strengthen the role of foreign and domestic capital in the urban industrial area. Through expropriation of the property of the old landowners and remuneration that had to be invested in new industry, the regime had endeavored to convert agrarian capitalists into industrial capitalists with the objective of eliminating dependency. Quijano showed that in fact, as the regime became more efficient and better organized, its ties to imperialist monopolies made it less national than before.

His analysis emphasized the relations among social classes. The Peruvian ruling class, for example, was perceived by Quijano as a dependent bourgeoisie but becoming more heterogeneous as a consequence of the declining power of the landowners and the growing importance of the urban industrial groups. Specifically, he saw the ruling class as comprising an upper landholding bourgeoisie, residing along the coast, responsible for agricultural exports and not directly controlled by foreign companies; a middle-level landowning bourgeoisie, located in the mountains and owners of agricultural resources producing for the domestic market; an upper industrial bourgeoisie dependent on foreign investment; and a middle industrial bourgeoisie with moderate financial resources. These sectors were bound by family and financial ties.

Given its attempt to restructure the ruling class and to promote involvement by the popular sectors in the Peruvian economy, the regime had believed that it could transcend capitalism and build in its stead a nationalist, humanist, and communitarian order that would preclude socialism. Quijano argued that this conception was an illusion—that the so-called new order had strengthened the dependent bourgeoisie and ensured an alliance between the dependent bourgeoisie and the imperialist bourgeoisie. He concluded that "there is absolutely no question here of eliminating imperialist investment . . . under the formal limits established by the law, the margins of imperialist participation are sufficient to assure it a dominant position in the country's economy, even though it may be subject to state supervision" (Quijano 1971, 73). He went on to argue that the state would also play a new role as an active participant in capitalist accumulation and would attempt to become dominant in the regulation of the economy. This situation would involve a reorganization of the financial apparatus of the state and its extension throughout the financial network of the country. Thus the prospects were poor for a regime whose ideology of limited nationalism placed it within the imperialist order:

> There is no nationalist anti-imperialist bourgeoisie in Latin America. What does exist is a small nationalist bourgeoisie which, in the absence of any real ability on the part of the dominated classes to exert pressure for its historic interests or to fight for power, is not likely to evolve a line of conduct capable of effectively eliminating imperialist domination. [Quijano 1971, 115]

In another work, Quijano (1974) focused specifically on imperialism in Latin America. He began with the assumption, expressed by Lenin, that under the control of finance capital, a monopolization of capital leads to imperialism and the need for international capital accumulation. Imperialist capitalist accumulation, however, has evolved in different ways in Latin America.

First, imperialism was evident during a period of semicolonial accumulation that lasted until the 1950s and was characterized by the concentration of imperialist capital in the production of primary products; the organization of enclaves connected to the metropolitan capitalist economy, not to the internal economy of a dependent country; the generation of surplus in the form of both surplus value from the enclaves and mercantile surplus from the precapitalist sector; and the accumulation in the imperialist countries of most of the surplus value created in the dominated country.

Within Latin America, this imperialism took different forms in different regions. For example, countries bordering the Atlantic—such as Mexico, Brazil, and Argentina—were closely integrated into the world market, and centers of capitalist production began to evolve from the "feudal-mercantile matrix" as "elements of the mercantile-capitalist bourgeoisie had managed to consolidate their hegemony over class and state." In contrast, the mercantilism that developed in other countries was stagnating, "feudal and semi-feudal relations of production had become prevalent, the economy had become predominantly agricultural, the domestic market was small, and urban centers were on the decline." Quijano suggested that the dependent national bourgeoisies of countries like Mexico, Brazil, and Argentina invested in domestic industry and gave the appearance that they advocated autonomous national and capitalist development and an independent foreign policy, whereas in the other Latin American countries, the bourgeoisie was "weak and dispersed, tied to the precapitalist and mercantilist landowners, and especially—through its feudalism—to the interests of the imperialist bourgeoisie." Thus all efforts to bring about autonomous national capitalist development were perceived by the bourgeoisie as a threat to its interests (Quijano 1974, 69–70).

Second, imperialism also evolved through a period of urban and industrial-based accumulation following the Second World War. In Mexico, Brazil, and Argentina, this massive expansion of imperialist capital resulted in the denationalization of control over capital, the integration of national and foreign capital, and the association of the national and imperialist bourgeoisies. Imperialist capital expanded rapidly while assimilating national capitalists into the enterprise of exploitation. Quijano described the consequences of this imperialist penetration as urban and industrial activity upon which accumulation is based; expansion and internationalization of the internal markets of the dominated countries; accumulation of surplus value to broaden the global base of production and reproduction of capital in the metropolitan economy; disappearance of the enclave; establishment of links between the urban-industrial economy and the metropolitan economy; and concentration of capital by the state and the national-imperialist and international corporations associated with the state. Recognition of these consequences helps in understanding "the unevenly combined character of these countries' capitalist structures" and the deepening of contradictions between capitalism and the remaining precapitalism; between the semicolonial mode of imperialist accumulation, with its national and imperialist base, and the new international mode of accumulation, involving the internationalization of expanded capitalist reproduction (Quijano 1974, 73–76).

Thus different types of nations entering the world imperialist system are identifiable, including those in which the semicolonial mode of imperialist accumulation is predominant and those in which this mode is combined with the new mode but the base does not allow incorporation into the internationalized expanded reproduction. The domination of imperialist capital results in the integration of finance with productive capital, the consolidation of the interests of the imperialist and national-imperialist bourgeoisies, and the replacement of old monopolistic businesses by giant conglomerates that combine vertical and horizontal integration. Finally, the national-imperialist states begin to defend not only their own interests but those of the global system as well (Quijano 1974, 73–76).

Quijano assessed these recent trends and concluded that the new imperialism tended to promote political crisis in Latin America. This crisis was related, first, to the intensification of class struggle, involving the declining power of the feudal-mercantile landowners and the growth of power of the new elements of the bourgeoisie, the expansion in numbers of the proletariat, and the expanding role of the intermediate classes. Second, "the uneven character of dependent capitalism" produced a crisis of political hegemony. Quijano said that "all modes of capitalist accumulation from the most primitive to the most recent exist in these countries, interconnecting, combining, and superimposing themselves on one another." As capitalism expanded, the new bourgeois sectors sought greater political power, sometimes by combining with intermediate sectors and even the proletariat. But in Latin America, these new bourgeois sectors did not always establish political hegemony, and the military thus became important: "In all of the countries in which the dominated classes had failed to reach a sufficient level of organization and political competence . . . the armed forces were well situated to take control of the state's administrative and repressive apparatus—given the political bankruptcy of the bourgeoisie and the political weakness of the dominated classes" (Quijano 1974, 86, 88). Third, there was the relative autonomization of the state, under the control of the military, bureaucracy, and business elements. Quijano believed that these groups constituted "a new power elite," a ruling class with clear interests: "to control and appropriate the vast resources at the disposal of state capitalism—in association with the large international monopolies" (Quijano 1974, 91).

Unlike most of the other thinkers whose ideas and works have been reviewed thus far, Quijano has succeeded rather well in relating the concept of dependency to the class interests of domestic capital and ties with international capital. His analysis focuses on modes of production through history and the class alliances and struggles that emanate from the penetration and impact of imperialism upon the less developed nations of Latin America. His framework allows for detailed examination of both internal and external class forces and for a realistic and an in-depth appraisal of political and economic developments in the area. In very clear terms he not only identifies categories of class but also relates these categories to the productive process, the growth of an economy affected by capitalism and imperialism, the conflict between old and new classes, the changing structure of institutional life, the pattern of hegemonic power, and the degree of capitalist accumulation and reproduction that takes place both in the outlying areas of the international capitalist system and in its metropolitan centers.

Of special significance is Quijano's emphasis upon a class analysis, particularly his effort to deal with the working class.[55] In addition, he has written extensively on the marginality of a substantial segment of the population in Latin America. In his early writings, he attempted to distinguish the notion of marginality from Marx's discussion of the plight of the reserve army of unemployed industrial workers by suggesting that the marginal population could never be absorbed into the productive process; later, however, he has emphasized the Marxist conception.[56] Quijano (1979) has also looked specifically at the role of peasants in the face of imperialism and efforts at agrarian reform in the less developed countries.

Any discussion of Quijano must conclude with some attention to his efforts to relate general theoretical discussion to an analysis of practical politics and of contemporary Peru. Recently, for example, he analyzed the impact of capitalism and imperialism upon the working class, the organization of the bourgeoisie and its class allies, and the prospects for a new popular movement (Quijano 1980). The crisis in the Peruvian economy, he believed, would lead to consciousness of their plight on the part of the impoverished small bourgeoisie and the disintegration that every crisis brings to the working class. He predicted that the political forces of the bourgeoisie and the intermediate strata would be reorganized to confront the emerging popular struggles in

Latin America against fascist and oligarchic military regimes; the result would be "controlled decompression" to ensure bourgeois hegemony while opening up the political system to some popular participation. Among the options available in this process were liberal authoritarianism, populist developmentalism, and social democracy. He went on to analyze the emerging popular movement and its strengths and weaknesses as it assumed a position that was fundamentally reformist in content and to discuss the prospects for revolutionary socialism.

The Legacy of Trotskyism: Vitale, Novack, and Mandel

Reference has been made to the contributions of Leon Trotsky relating to ideas about development and underdevelopment. Many thinkers have carried on in this tradition. Several of the early writers on dependency and underdevelopment once were associated with Trotskyist intellectuals or movements, including Silvio Frondizi, Theotonio dos Santos, Ruy Mauro Marini, and Aníbal Quijano. In particular, the notions of center and periphery, dependency and dependent capitalist development continue to be used in this line of thinking.[57] Three additional writers merit discussion: Luis Vitale, George Novack, and Ernest Mandel.

Luis Vitale was born in Argentina in 1927 and later became a naturalized citizen of Chile, where he became renowned as a writer and professor of history and geography. Prior to the 1973 military coup, he had been associated with the University of Concepción. He had also been involved in various Trotskyist movements affiliated with the Fourth International and had served as the national director of the labor organization Central Unica de Trabajadores de Chile (CUT) from 1959 to 1962. He was responsible for writing two pamphlets for the first and second national congresses of CUT in 1957 and 1959, and he contributed other assessments of the Chilian labor movement.[58] After the 1973 coup he went into exile in West Germany. His principal writings fall into two areas, one dealing with the questions of whether Latin America is feudal or capitalist; the other, with a Marxist interpretation of Chilean history.

On the question of feudalism or capitalism, Vitale argued against the widely accepted premises that feudalism was transplanted from medieval Spain to the New World and that a feudal aristocracy had emerged in Latin America and continued to rule until the twentieth century, thus blocking capitalism and the rise of a national bourgeoisie (Vitale 1968, 1971a; also Glausser R. and Vitale 1974). Vitale believed that these premises were associated with the political movements led by Getúlio Vargas in Brazil, Juan Perón in Argentina, and social democratic parties in Chile, Peru, and Venezuela. "The concept of feudal Spain has taken on special significance in the present century. Its standard-bearers are the pseudo-leftist sociologists and politicians who confuse economic *backwardness* with feudalism or *latifundium* with feudalism" (Vitale 1968, 33).

He argued that feudalism had embedded itself in Spain during the ninth to the twelfth centuries and declined thereafter. A natural economy was transformed into a monetary economy as Spain moved through the transition from feudalism to capitalism. Only a primitive capitalism existed during the fifteenth century. The conquest and colonization of the Americas were associated with the objective of exploitation and commercialization of precious metals. Thus Spain conquered the Americas with the intent, not of reproducing European feudalism, but of incorporating the new area into a system of capitalist production. Spanish America was ruled, not by feudal lords, but by a commercial bourgeoisie whose source of wealth was exports. Since independence, the ruling bourgeoisie has remained dependent on the world market, which has contributed to the backwardness of the continent. "Dependent from the beginning on imperialism because of its own inability to develop heavy industry, it has exhausted all the possibilities for the development of a semicolonial society in an imperialist period" (Vitale 1968, 42).

This line of thinking underlies Vitale's *Interpretación marxista de la historia de Chile* (1967, 1971b), a grand synthesis of Chilean history from the country's pre-Hispanic origins to the nineteenth century and a monumental effort to demonstrate the consequences of imperialism. The Chilean socialist Julio César Jobet considered this work "a brilliant contribution to the clarification of the true objectives and position of the revolutionary movement" (Jobet, in Vitale 1967, 15).

George Novack, one of the leading theoreticians of the U.S. Socialist Workers party and the Fourth International, has generally written on philosophy and political theory, but he also shows the relationship of Trotskyist thought to the thesis, expressed in the work of Vitale, that backwardness in Latin America is a consequence of capitalism. One article by Novack consists of responses to a series of questions addressed to him by a Mexican Trotskyist organization (Novack 1970). First, he expressed concern about the extreme irregularity of world capitalist development, with capitalist power and economy concentrated in Western Europe and the United States and the rest of the world confined to backwardness.

> The stifling, stunting, and mangling forms of bourgeois life and labor, yoked together with archaic precapitalist relations, prevented the bourgeois strata, which had performed such progressive services in

revolutionizing the old order in Western Europe and the United States, from filling a comparable historical role in the colonized areas. [Novack 1970, 978]

Thus the most backward and the most modern forms of economic activity and exploitation are found in variable forms in different countries, but they may be locked together or combined in their social development, especially under the impact of imperialism. Under imperialism, the socialist world revolution will not occur simultaneously or instantly, but instead will evolve through a process in which the links of the imperialist chain are broken. Thus underdeveloped countries like Russia, Yugoslavia, China, Cuba, and Vietnam were able to break with the capitalist system, and ultimately other nations will wage victorious socialist revolutions.

Novack argued that the law of uneven and combined development was "a general law of the whole historical process of which the theory of permanent revolution is a particular expression limited to the period of transition from the capitalist system to socialism" (Novack 1970, 978). The problem in a single backward country is that although socialist forces might be victorious, such a revolution might not necessarily achieve its aims and program unless the workers also take power in the more industrialized areas of the world.

> Without a vigilant, firm, and highly conscious political leadership and, above all, without breaking the imperialist encirclement through the extension of proletarian power to the advanced countries, the backward workers' states run the risk of suffering retrogression and deformation along bureaucratic lines. The record of the Soviet regime under Stalin and his successors is the most forceful and appalling evidence of this danger. [Novack 1970, 979]

These themes of permanent revolution and combined and uneven development have been elaborated and analyzed by Michael Lowy (1981).

Does the idea of combined and uneven development run counter to the thesis of capitalist underdevelopment in the writing of André Gunder Frank? Frank had said it did, but Novack denied this statement. Novack explained that with the spread of capitalism, a world market had evolved and capitalism had confronted and penetrated all forms of precapitalist formations and relations; yet many of these precapitalist formations persisted. Although Frank had argued that Latin America had been essentially capitalist since the sixteenth century, Novack countered that such a "sweeping assertion cannot stand up against the historical facts or the method of Marxism" (Novack 1970, 980). He said that the capitalist mode of production had not fully established itself even in Europe until the nineteenth century and that at the time of the conquest of Latin America, Spain was as much feudal as bourgeois and therefore created economic forms with a combined character in the New World: "They welded precapitalist relations to exchange relations, thereby subordinating them to the demands and movements of merchant capital" (Novack 1970, 981).

Thus, he believed, Frank was wrong because he failed to distinguish between merchant capital and a mature or an industrial capitalist system; he focused on relations in the sphere of exchange and ignored those in production; he did not understand the combined and uneven formation found in the period of transition from a precapitalist to a full capitalist economy; and he did not consider the possibility of a coexistence of feudalism and capitalism. In short, Frank's approach "is highly oversimplified. It leaves no room for complex historical situations, combined class relations and contradictory socioeconomic formations" (Novack 1970, 981). Thus Novack distinguished his position from that of liberal scholars who wrote about the purely feudal past of Latin America and other backward areas in contrast to the democratic and modern development of the West. Likewise, he differed from the Moscow-oriented Communists who advocated alliance with the national bourgeoisie against landed interests and therefore, in his view, subordinated or sacrificed the revolutionary class struggle for workers' power.

Many of these assumptions underlie the thinking of the Belgian economist Ernest Mandel.[59] Mandel's writings clearly synthesize the conceptualizations of Marx, Lenin, and Trotsky and relate them to the contemporary world.[60] They also polemically contend with other points of view and focus on vital issues of capitalism and its impact everywhere.[61] Mandel has attempted to update Marxism in his overview of capitalism since the Second World War; this major synthesis, entitled *Late Capitalism* (1975), attempts to apply the general theory of "laws of motion" of the capitalist mode of production, as set forth by Marx, to the postwar period of boom and subsequent decline and of intensified class struggle during the seventies.[62]

Mandel's fundamental position regarding capitalist development and underdevelopment is clearly stated in a discussion of surplus profit. Referring to the uneven and combined development of states, regions, and industry, Mandel identified a whole system of development and underdevelopment in which the parts are reciprocal to each other so that surplus in the form of profit is achieved at the expense of less developed countries and regions (Mandel called them colonies and semicolonies). "Hence development takes place only in juxtaposition with underdevelopment; it perpetuates the latter and itself develops thanks to this perpetuation" (Mandel 1975, 102; for critical reviews, see Block 1977 and Cypher 1977). Mandel insisted that there could have been no transfer of surplus to industrialized regions without underdeveloped regions, for the capitalist world system is an integrated and a hierarchized whole of development and underdevelopment that has taken different forms in different epochs.

> In the age of freely competitive capitalism its predominant weight lay in the regional juxtaposition of development and underdevelopment. In the age of classical imperialism it lay in the international juxtaposition of development in the imperialist states and underdevelopment in the colonial and semicolonial countries. In the age of late capitalism it lies in the overall industrial juxtaposition of development in growth sectors and underdevelopment in others, primarily in the imperialist countries but also in the semicolonies in a secondary way. [Mandel 1975, 103]

Surplus profits, he believed, were quantitatively more important than unequal exchange both before the First World War and during the interwar period. In those periods, the metropolitan areas drew primarily upon colonial surplus profits as the chief form of exploitation of the Third World. During the late capitalist period, unequal exchange became the main form of exploitation.[63] There was a shift in the movement of capital exports between metropolitan states rather than from them to the colonies, and there was also a shift of foreign investment from extraction of raw materials to the manufacture of consumer goods. Mandel saw that nationalist and anti-imperialist movements within the less developed countries had often made it more difficult to transfer profits to the metropolitan countries and that the colonial bourgeoisies had attempted to increase their share of the surplus value produced by workers and peasants. Likewise, the developing multinational firms sought to dominate the small and slowly growing internal markets of the colonies, thereby interfering with the role of the national bourgeoisies in dominating the manufacturing industry. Combinations of national and foreign as well as of private and public capital thus became a feature of the late capitalist phase of imperialism.

Mandel identified basic sources of unequal exchange in the capitalist world economy and then exposed weaknesses in the theses of Raúl Prebisch and Samir Amin, who had sought clarity "with the aid of an eclectic theory combining Marx and Ricardo and detouring through wage costs, even though it can be resolved quite satisfactorily and directly within the context of Marx's theory of value and surplus-value" (Mandel 1975, 351–352). Mandel also criticized Arghiri Emmanuel for using "an eclectic theory of value and an uncritical manipulation of macroeconomic aggregates . . . to question the whole Leninist theory of imperialism by refuting the very existence of an increasing export of capital in search of colonial surplus-profits from the imperialist countries to the colonies and semicolonies before the First World War" (Mandel 1975, 355). He agreed with Charles Bettelheim that one must start with relations of production and differences in productivity in order to show the different developmental trends in metropolitan and colonial countries and acknowledged that his attention to the "productivity differential that does not precede capitalism but is produced by it" allows a focus on the accumulation of capital on a world scale. Mandel agreed with Emmanuel and Amin that the "problem of 'unequal exchange' ultimately goes back to the problem of the different social structure of the underdeveloped countries" (Mandel 1975, 365). He also agreed with André Gunder Frank that capitalism in the center appropriates surplus and thus produces underdevelopment in the less developed countries, but he identified differences with Frank, especially in his analysis of mechanisms that stimulate dependency:

> He sees them in the capitalist nature of the economy of these colonies and semi-colonies (which he confuses with subordination to the capitalist world market); we see them in the specific combination of pre-capitalist, semi-capitalist, and capitalist relations of production which characterizes the social structure of these countries. . . . it is precisely the relations of production which would need to be included in his analysis, to grasp the mechanisms of the "development of underdevelopment" which block disintegration of pre-capitalist and semi-capitalist relations of production precisely by the specific form of their integration into the world market. Because he does not take social relations of production into account, however, Frank is unable to explain why the extension of commodity production for export in the colonies and semi-colonies has not set in motion the same cumulative process of capital accumulation and capitalist production as occurred in the imperialist countries. [Mandel 1975, 365–366]

This glimpse into the thought of Mandel allows for some understanding of the Trotskyist thesis of uneven and combined development and its relevance to exchange theories about development and underdevelopment. Mandel identified with important ideas in Amin, Emmanuel, and Frank that allowed him to see a reciprocal relationship between development and underdevelopment. He wrote of dependent relationships and attributed development in the advanced capitalist countries to the exploitation of capitalism and imperialism in the underdeveloped areas. That exploitation took the form of extraction of surplus profit and its transfer to the industrialized countries during the period before the Second World War. Thereafter, unequal exchange, involving the underdeveloped countries and their ties to the international market, characterized this exploitation. Mandel accepted Frank's thesis of capitalist underdevelopment but found fault with its inattention to precapitalist, semicapitalist, and capitalist relations of production. Without analysis of these relations of production, he argued, one could not adequately understand the process of underdevelopment.

5 / Capitalist Underdevelopment and Circulationist Views of the World System

An emphasis in the writings on underdevelopment that relates closely to and parallels the socialist and revolutionary tradition originated with the economist Paul Baran, who analyzed a variety of meanings of the term "surplus" and linked backwardness to the impact of capitalism in the less developed parts of the world. Influenced by Baran, André Gunder Frank elaborated the thesis of capitalist development and underdevelopment, that is, the idea that the diffusion of capitalism into the outlying areas tends to create underdevelopment rather than promote development. Associated with this idea was the notion that Latin America, undeveloped before the conquest, has experienced underdevelopment since the sixteenth century because of the capitalism that penetrated the New World. The tendency of writers to divide the world into center and periphery was adopted by Immanuel Wallerstein, who offered an interpretive history of capitalist development in Europe since the fifteenth century. Arghiri Emmanuel analyzed relations of exchange in an effort to extend the earlier treatment of Marx, and Samir Amin incorporated concepts like underdevelopment and dependency as well as center and periphery into his focus on accumulation and unequal development on a world scale. All these writers looked at patterns of trade in the international political economy; they were concerned with the circulation of merchant capital and the impact of the dominant world capitalist system upon the peripheral areas.

The Roots of Backwardness: Baran

Paul Baran (1910–1964) was born in Russia, lived part of his life in Poland, and studied in Berlin, Frankfurt, and Paris before going to the United States in 1939 to continue his studies at Harvard University and the Brookings Institution. Later he became professor of economics at Stanford University and one of the few Marxist social scientists then teaching at a major U.S. university. Baran was especially known for his writings on backwardness and monopoly capitalism, among them *The*

Political Economy of Growth (1960), *The Longer View* (1969), and a collaborative essay with Paul Sweezy, *Monopoly Capital* (1966).[64]

Baran was concerned about the impact of monopoly capitalism on the individual and society. In particular, he examined the injustice and irrationality of capitalism in underdeveloped countries, and he believed that Marxism was relevant to an understanding of this condition. According to John O'Neill, Baran "never faltered in his sense of the relevance of Marxism to the understanding of interdependencies between the fate of the individual under monopoly capitalism and the birth of the individual in countries lying in the shadow of Western imperialism" (O'Neill 1969, xxiii). Baran felt that Marx in the nineteenth century and later Lenin, Rudolf Hilferding, Rosa Luxemburg, and others had accurately portrayed the tendency of capitalism to evolve into stagnation, imperialism, and political crisis (Baran 1960).

He argued that socialism in the advanced countries would eventually serve humanity. He favored a socialism that "would not only attack head-on the waste, irrationality, and cultural and moral degradation of the West," but also "throw its weight into helping to solve the entire problem of want, disease, and starvation in the underdeveloped parts of the world" (Baran 1960, ix).[65] Socialism in the West, he believed, must avoid the political and social repression that had accompanied the early stages of socialism in the East, and socialism in backward and underdeveloped countries must overcome "a powerful tendency to become a backward and underdeveloped socialism" (Baran 1960, viii).

Throughout his writings, Baran emphasized the nature of underdeveloped countries: "The backward world has always represented the indispensable hinterland of the highly developed capitalist West" (Baran 1960, 12). These countries were also dependent, for Baran equated colonialism with dependency in the contemporary world and argued that the dependent countries could not achieve accumulation as the advanced countries had or overcome the obstacles of monopoly capitalism and imperialism.

This concern with underdevelopment also led Baran to attack proponents of capitalist development as a way out of backwardness. In particular, he exposed the weaknesses in W. W. Rostow's *The Stages of Economic Growth: A Non-Communist Manifesto* (1960). Rostow had examined economic growth within historical periods and argued that growth was a discontinuous and dialectical process until a takeoff stage of self-sustained advancement was reached. Baran criticized this conception by suggesting that

> Rostovian stage theory, despite its comprehensive historic and sociological claims, reduces economic growth to a single pattern. . . .

within its extremely narrow limits the Rostovian theory can neither explain nor predict without introducing considerations that are completely irrelevant to the stage schema. . . . An examination of the principal tenets of Rostow's theory of economic growth . . . thus reveals nothing that can be considered an addition to our knowledge of the history of economic development or an enrichment of our understanding of the processes involved. [Baran 1969, xxiii]

Beyond his criticism of non-Marxist economics, Baran attempted to set forth his own theoretical formulation about underdevelopment. Four concepts are essential to this theory: underconsumption, economic surplus, backwardness, and monopoly capital. Baran was critical of most writings on underconsumption, but he considered the concept of underconsumption important for an understanding of the capitalist system.[66] He argued for a refinement of the concept that would distinguish its useful from its wasteful components. He felt that inquiry was called for in situations in which, because of a rise in investment, effective demand would be insufficient for a full use of resources. He noted that since the turn of the century there had been a significant rise in productivity, output, and economic surplus. Consequently, "this economic surplus tends to be continually redistributed in favor of a steadily decreasing number of giant capitalist enterprises." Rather than resulting in chronic depression, this situation was corrected—in the competitive phase of capitalism by price cutting so as to ensure a reduction of economic surplus and in the phase of monopoly capitalism by an increase in waste and unproductive labor (for example, expansion of sales organizations, advertising campaigns, public relations campaigns, and lobbying efforts). "The results of this development," according to Baran, "are a rampant growth of the system's unproductive sector and a striking multiplication of waste" (Baran 1969, 192). This position led him to the meaning of the concept of economic surplus.

Baran distinguished three kinds of economic surplus.[67] First, actual economic surplus is "the difference between society's *actual* current output and its *actual* current consumption." He suggested that this type of surplus is the same as current saving or accumulation as represented in productive facilities and equipment, inventories, and so on. Actual economic surplus composes a lesser share of total output than Marx's surplus value—actual economic surplus "is merely that part of surplus value that is being *accumulated*: it does not include, in other words, the consumption of the capitalist class, the government's spending on administration, military establishment, and the like."

Second, potential economic surplus is "the difference between the output that *could* be produced in a given natural and technological environment with the help of employable productive resources, and what might be regarded as essential consumption." Baran distinguished potential economic surplus from Marx's surplus value: "On the one hand, it *excludes* such elements of surplus value as what was called above essential consumption of capitalists, what could be considered *essential* outlays on government administration and the like; on the other hand, it comprises what is not covered by the concept of surplus value—the output lost in view of unemployment or misemployment of productive resources." The realization of potential economic surplus could be brought about through a reorganization of production and distribution of social output so as to deal with four areas: excess consumption by upper-income groups; output lost through unproductive workers; output lost through wasteful organization of the productive apparatus; and output lost to unemployment. Baran elaborated on the nature of each of these areas.

Finally, he defined planned economic surplus as "the difference between society's 'optimum' output attainable in a historically given natural and technological environment under conditions of planned 'optimal' utilization of all available productive resources, and some chosen 'optimal' volume of consumption." Planned economic surplus would be based, not on the pressures of the capitalist order, but on the rational planning of a socialist society. These uses of economic surplus allowed Baran to delve into the question of backwardness.

Baran believed that it was necessary to understand "the laws of motion of both the advanced and backward parts of the capitalist world."[68] He wished to characterize all underdeveloped countries and to explain their condition of underdevelopment. He examined, in particular, the impact of two centuries of capitalism on India and concluded that the result was backwardness.

> It should not be overlooked that India, if left to herself, might have found in the course of time a shorter and surely less tortuous road toward a better and richer society. That on that road she would have had to pass through the purgatory of a bourgeois revolution, that a long phase of capitalist development would have been the inevitable price that she would have had to pay for progress. . . . It would have been, however, an entirely different India (and an entirely different world), had she been allowed—as some more fortunate countries were—to realize her destiny in her own way, to employ her resources for her own benefit, to harness her energies and abilities for the advancement of her own people. [Baran 1960, 150]

Baran believed that if the advanced capitalist countries had cooperated with and assisted rather than exploited and oppressed the backward world, then progressive development would have occurred. Instead, "the violent, destructive, and predatory opening up of the weaker countries by Western capitalism immeasurably distorted their development" (Baran 1960, 162).

In a work on the United States and monopoly capitalism today, Baran and Paul Sweezy argued that although Lenin had advanced Marxist theory with his emphasis on imperialism as the monopoly stage of capitalism, the task of analyzing monopoly in the context of the laws of motion of the underlying capitalist economy remained. Neither Marx nor Engels had fully incorporated monopoly into Marxian economic theory. Baran and Sweezy attempted to move in this direction by studying the generation and absorption of economic surplus, which they defined as "the difference between what a society produces and the costs of producing it" (Baran and Sweezy 1966, 9).[69] Their attention to monopoly, they admitted, neglected the labor process.

Their study focused on the giant corporation, in which they saw real power resting with management—"the insiders, those who devote full time to the corporation and whose interests and careers are tied to its fortunes" (Baran and Sweezy 1966, 16). They saw management as a self-perpetuating entity, each generation of managers recruiting and training its successors. They also noted that each corporation seeks financial independence through the generation of its own capital so that it is not necessary to use financial or bank capital to meet needs. This emphasis on corporate capital rather than financial capital distinguishes their analysis from that of Lenin and others fifty years earlier. They summarized their position:

> Business is an ordered system which selects and rewards according to well understood criteria. The guiding principle is to get as near as possible to the top inside a corporation which is as near as possible to top corporations. Hence the need for maximum profits. Hence the need to devote profits once acquired to enhancing financial strength and speeding up growth. . . . The real capitalist today is not the individual businessman but the corporation. [Baran and Sweezy 1966, 42–43]

In conclusion, Baran and Sweezy expressed concern about their treatment of monopoly capitalism: "If we confine attention to the inner dynamics of advanced monopoly capitalism, it is hard to avoid the conclusion that the prospect of effective revolutionary action to overthrow the system is slim. . . . advanced monopoly capitalism does not exist in isolation, and any speculation about its future which takes account only of its inner laws and tendencies is certain to be misleading"

(Baran and Sweezy 1966, 364–365). They suggested a revolutionary outcome as the prevalent form of resistance to the world capitalist system and of struggle for a socialist basis; the victories of China, Algeria, Cuba, Vietnam and Korea are examples of how revolutionary peoples have attempted to solve their problems within the world capitalist system, because the United States will resist the increasing commitment and advance of the world revolution: "The drama of our time is the world revolution; it can never come to an end until it has encompassed the whole world" (Baran and Sweezy 1966, 367).

Toward the end of his life, Baran was able to visit Cuba and observe the accomplishments of the socialist experiment there. Reflecting on the Cuban Revolution, he advanced a number of propositions. First, it followed no preconceived scheme; Cuban intellectuals and revolutionary leaders reported that it had "grown spontaneously, owing its methods, its direction, and its triumph to specific conditions in Cuba as well as to the genius of Fidel Castro."[70] Second, it was not merely a political revolution, but a social one that had profoundly changed the socioeconomic structure of the country, its economic relations, and the ownership of the means of production. Third, it was brought about, not by the young intellectuals, but by the rural population, which was "driven to revolt by the increasingly insufferable state of poverty, exploitation, and backwardness to which it was condemned by the old order. Its success in making the Revolution and the direction it gave the Revolution were largely determined by its economic, social, and ideological structure" (Baran 1969, 395). In elaborating on this position, Baran argued that Cuban agriculture had become at an early stage an appendage of monopoly capital; it had not evolved into a feudal system. Thus the Cuban peasants "fought not for the ownership of the soil they tilled, but for essentially working class objectives: steady employment, more human working conditions, and more adequate wages" (Baran 1969, 397).

Baran then looked at the revolution itself and offered some observations about its uniqueness: Because sugar grows prolifically, the potential economic surplus in Cuba was substantial, and vast areas of uncultivated land could be placed in production with moderate investment. Further, Cuba was able to feed itself, unlike other countries that had experienced socialist revolution in the face of food shortage. This fact suggested that industrial enterprise could be readily established: "In a short time it can radically increase and diversify its agricultural output. . . . Becoming thus self-sufficient with regard to food, it can devote the foreign exchange proceeds of its exports to the acquisition of machinery, oil, and those raw materials and consumer goods which it is impossible, or at least at the present time uneconomical, to produce at home" (Baran 1969, 411). He concluded optimistically that Cuba could bring about a most profound transformation: "the transition from capitalism to socialism—with a minimum of repression and with a minimum of violence, in an atmosphere of freedom and enthusiastic participation of a resurrected nation" (Baran 1969, 412). At the same time, he warned that U.S. policies and actions related to Cuba (in particular, the Bay of Pigs invasion) threatened to bring about world collapse: "The issue is not even capitalism or socialism . . . [but] world survival or a world catastrophe" (Baran 1969, 436).

The writings of Baran inspired a plethora of ideas around the notion that capitalism leads to underdevelopment and dependency in the peripheral areas of the world. André Gunder Frank and Samir Amin were just two of a host of writers who elaborated on this provocative thesis. Although their ideas were enthusiastically received and accepted by much of the academic community, especially in U.S. universities, a critical assessment was also offered.

Anthony Brewer argued that Baran had contributed to an important shift in Marxist theory, especially in the emphasis on monopoly capital as the cause of stagnation in both advanced and underdeveloped countries. He was also "the first major Marxist theorist to treat under-developed countries as worthy of study in their own right." He differed from other scholars in his view that capitalism functions differently in underdeveloped countries than in advanced countries. Overall, his "approach has become fundamental to subsequent Marxist thinking about underdevelopment. . . . there is a consistent development, starting very close to classical Marxism, but evolving into something distinctly different" (Brewer 1980, 132–133). Brewer concluded by saying that Baran's theory of monopoly capital leads to "a static argument applied to an essentially dynamic problem"; that his treatment of economic surplus takes him back to a classical position worked out before Marx; and that his work "represents a move towards seeing capitalist devel-opment as the development of one area at the expense of others. Ultimately this can lead to a view of history as a zero sum game, a struggle for the division of a fixed world income" (Brewer 1980, 148). Finally, Brewer felt that Baran's importance is in "having directed Marxists' attention to the analysis of underdeveloped countries, and in having provided many of the ideas that were built on by subsequent writers" (Brewer 1980, 157).

A less sympathetic and more penetrating critique is found in a review by James Cypher of the work of Baran. Cypher called the development of underdevelopment arguments "ahistorical, static, and exchanged-based. . . . The foundation of their model of a static reproduction of underdevelopment [was] perpetuated by an equilibrium of socio-economic forces" (Cypher 1979, 35). John Taylor went a step further in his examination of the underdevelopment theory of Baran and Frank: "Their discourse contains serious explanatory limitations which ultimately render it theoretically untenable" (Taylor 1979, 71). Taylor argued that Baran failed to analyze any particular mode of production as is necessary in examining capitalism in the less developed countries.

> The absence of any real analysis of non-capitalist modes, combined with the absence of any analysis of different forms of capitalist penetration of these modes leads Baran to the inadequate conclusion that his penetration simply "blocked" the evolution of capitalism. From this follows the corollary that economic development *per se* is predicated on a removal of this penetration. This argument then becomes the foundation for a simplistic opposition that reduces the theoretical analysis of an underdeveloped society to a description of how the surplus that is produced is utilized. [Taylor 1979, 83]

Capitalist Development of Underdevelopment: André Gunder Frank and Walter Rodney

André Gunder Frank was born in Berlin in 1929, received his doctorate in economics from the University of Chicago (where he researched questions on Soviet agriculture), and taught at various universities in the United States, Canada, England, and Germany. He first visited Latin America in 1962, remaining for four years teaching sociological theory at the University of Brasília and economic development at the national universities of Chile and Mexico. In an article published in 1966, Frank argued that most "theory fails to explain the structure and development of the capitalist system as a whole and to account for its simultaneous generation of underdevelopment in some of its parts and of economic development in others." He criticized the view that economic development takes place through a succession of stages and that underdeveloped countries today may pass through higher stages of development: "Underdevelopment is not original or traditional. . . . The now developed countries were never *under*developed, though they may have been *un*developed" (Frank 1966, 17, 18).

Frank advanced a series of hypotheses. First, a relationship of metropoles to satellites exists in the world today that means that the metropoles tend to develop and the satellites to underdevelop. The world metropolis is all-embracing and not the satellite of any entity, whereas the development of national and other subordinate metropoles is limited by their satellite status. This relationship is illustrated by dependent national metropoles such as Buenos Aires and São Paulo, which began to grow in the nineteenth century but today remain dependent on the outside metropoles of Great Britain and the United States. Second, satellites develop when ties to metropoles are weakest, for example, during wars and depressions in the world metropolis. Five crises exemplify this situation: the European depression of the seventeenth century, the Napoleonic Wars, the First World War, the Great Depression of 1932, and the Second World War. However, once the metropolis recovers from its crisis, the satellites tend to become reabsorbed into the world system, and consequently, the earlier development is stifled and unable to reproduce itself. Third, areas that now appear to be feudal and backward were once in fact, not isolated and precapitalist, but able to provide primary products and a large source of capital to the world metropolis. Once these areas were abandoned by the metropolis, they fell into decline. Fourth, in underdeveloped areas, the latifundium, or large estate, was established as a commercial enterprise in response to the demands of national and world markets. Fifth, the backward and feudal-like character of some latifundia is the consequence, not of their isolation, but of the decline of agricultural and mining areas abandoned by the world metropolis (Frank 1966, 23–30).

The basis of these theses on underdevelopment is found in one of the early writings of Frank, *On Capitalist Development* (1975b), prepared during October and November 1963 in Rio de Janeiro. This essay is broken into three parts. The first sets forth the argument that before development, there was no underdevelopment: "Underdevelopment as we know it today, and economic development as well, are the simultaneous and related products of the development . . . of a single integrated economic system: capitalism" (Frank 1975b, 43). Here Frank emphasizes economic surplus in the process of development and underdevelopment, relying upon the use of that concept by Paul Baran and upon some empirical evidence identifying actual economic surplus presented by Raúl Prebisch. The second part delves into the historical nature of underdevelopment, departing from Baran's essays on backwardness and Marx's analysis of the British devastation of India during the nineteenth century. The third elaborates on specific issues arising from interpretations of capitalist underdevelopment: feudalisms, mercantilism, internal colonialism, and so on. In this work, Frank argued that for more than four centuries, capitalism had shaped a single historical process and the development of one integrated system on a world scale. One part of the system exploits another, and regional differences appear: "Although there results a regional concentration of development and underdevelopment, there also develop developed sectors in underdeveloped regions and underdeveloped sectors in developed regions as the products of the same process of uneven capitalist development" (Frank 1975b, 43).

This and other early essays, including one on the links between metropole and satellite in a study of underdevelopment in Chile, written in 1964; one on internal colonialism and the Indian problem, prepared in 1965; and another on Brazil, set down shortly thereafter, were incorporated into his *Capitalism and Underdevelopment in Latin America*, published in 1967. In the preface to this work, Frank credited Paul Baran with helping him understand the obstacles to development of underdeveloped societies. He says that he had thought of himself as a progressive "liberal" until he became aware of the need to go to the underdeveloped countries "to learn *political* science and political economy in the classical pre-liberal and the Marxian post-liberal sense" (Frank 1967, xiv). He emphasized three "contradictions" in the capitalist underdevelopment of Latin America: that of monopolistic expropriation and appropriation by capitalists of economic surplus created by producers or workers; that of polarization into a metropolitan center and peripheral satellites; and that of the continuity of the capitalist system and its creation of underdevelopment (Frank 1967, 6–14).

In the case of Chile, Frank argued that economic cycles generated by the development of capitalism on a world scale determined the relative economic isolation of Chile from the metropolis. During the seventeenth century, Chile "had already been more isolated or more weakly integrated into the world capitalist metropolis-satellite structure than other Spanish colonies." During the eighteenth century, Chile continued to be essentially export oriented, first with gold and silver and later copper, while during the nineteenth century, capitalism consolidated underdevelopment within the country: "The fundamental capitalist contradictions . . . frustrated Chile's attempts at national development and condemned its people to the continued development of underdevelopment." During the present century, the contradictions deepened as Chile's dependence on the United States increased. He concluded that Chilean underdevelopment was not the consequence of a feudal structure, that domestic power had always been tied to foreign commercial interests, and that the state and its institutions had "always been part and parcel of the capitalist system in Chile and in the world and an instrument of the bourgoisie" (Frank 1967, 33, 36, 55, 116).

Frank presented a somewhat similar analysis of capitalist underdevelopment in Brazil. He attacked as "factually erroneous and theoretically inadequate and misleading" the argument that Brazil is dualist, that is, part modern and capitalist, part precapitalist, feudal or semifeudal

(Frank 1967, 146); he advanced an alternative model that envisaged a chain from the world metropolis to international satellites like São Paulo to provincial metropolises like Belo Horizonte and Recife and their regional and local satellites. He illustrated this model by referring to the rise and decline of the sugar industry and the underdevelopment of the Northeast; in his view, the sugar industry as a national metropolis stimulated a satellite economy of its own in the form of livestock raising.

> Livestock was used for meat, for hides, for draft animals to run the sugar mills, for fat to grease their works, for beasts of burden to carry the huge quantities of firewood used in the boilers. . . . The stockmen were exploited by the sugar mills whose satellite they were. . . . The satellite livestock economy formed a metropolis in turn with respect to the Indian zones into which its expansion forced the Indians to withdraw. . . . The European metropolis thus affected the life of the interior through a long chain of metropolises and satellites. [Frank 1967, 154]

Frank also examined the destruction of Portuguese textile industries, the consequence of the 1703 Treaty of Methuen whereby Portugal became an exporter of wine in exchange for British textiles, which in turn flooded the Portuguese market. Portugal became an intermediary between Great Britain and Brazil and other Portuguese colonies, "a satellite-metropolis which took an ever smaller part of the economic surplus of its own Brazilian satellite thanks to the political monopoly position it still retained, while Great Britain took over the economic monopoly and spoils" (Frank 1967, 156).

Beyond this pioneering effort to elaborate on a theory of under-development, Frank also devoted considerable attention to criticism of other writers, examples of which are collected in *Latin America: Underdevelopment or Revolution* (1969). Here Frank restated his thesis that underdevelopment is the consequence of world capitalist devel-opment and attempted to expose the ideological basis upon which both reactionary conservative and progressive liberal thinking rest. First, he systematically attacked the ideal-typical index approach rep-resented by Max Weber's conception of ideal types and Talcott Parson's pattern variables—found later in the writings of Bert Hoselitz, the stages-of-growth approach of W. W. Rostow, and the view of U.S. economists that the knowledge, technology, and capital of developed countries can be diffused to underdeveloped ones.[71] Second, he offered a rebuttal to the views of economist Robert Heilbroner on U.S. poli-cymaking.[72] Third, he exposed the liberal inclinations and the close ties of anthropologists to U.S. security agencies.[73] Frank also examined the mechanisms of imperialism, in particular the impact of U.S. aid on Latin America, the flow of capital from Brazil to the United States, the futility of economic integration schemes in Latin America, and the weaknesses of U.S. foreign policy. In addition, he turned his attention to criticism of such progressive thinkers as Pablo González Casanova, whose emphasis on a dual society, internal colonialism, and precapitalism Frank considered "empirically erroneous, theoretically illogical, and consequently, scientifically totally unacceptable,"[74] and Celso Furtado, whose reformism Frank felt implied "preventing revolution."[75] Finally, Frank moved toward a solution to capitalist underdevelopment, suggesting that the immediate enemy of national liberation was the national bourgeoisie and imperialism, the class structure in underdeveloped areas was formed by the colonial structure of international capitalism, and an anti-imperialist struggle could only be a class struggle.[76]

These attacks on other social scientists were quickly challenged, and, in response, Frank acknowledged some of the problems in his work.[77] A group of Mexican critics had argued that Frank's histcrical analysis lacked depth and that he failed to emphasize social classes. Frank defended his earlier work by claiming that he indeed understood underdevelopment in terms of classes, especially the bourgeoisie. Frank went on to show how the policies of the bourgeoisie strengthen economic dependence and perpetuate the development of underdevelopment; he called such a bourgeoisie the "lumpen bourgeoisie" and the underdevelopment generated by its activities "lumpen development." He also attempted to give the term "dependence" an operational definition, though he considered it "no more than a euphemism that cloaks subjection, oppression, alienation, and imperialist, capitalist racism, all of which are *internal* as well as external" (Frank 1972, 9). He also continued to use the term "underdevelopment," although he viewed its current usage as "the most shameless negation—ideological, political, economic, social, cultural, and psychological—of an accurate conception of reality" (Frank 1972, 9).

The intensity of the criticism and debate about the ideas of Frank cannot be underestimated. Frank himself provided an indication of this reaction in an article that specifically answered more than one hundred critics. He suggested that these critics represented three major tendencies: the backward-looking right (conservative, liberal, and social democratic), the traditional Marxist left, and the forward-looking new left. He suggested that "the importance of the dependence theory of underdevelopment is undeniable" but that changing world conditions involving declining rates of growth, profits, and investment mean that dependence "has ended or is completing the cycle of its natural life, at least in the Latin America that gave it birth" (Frank 1977a, 357; also 1974b).

Clearly, the onslaught against Frank pressured him to turn in an apparently new direction. Frank has described the shaping of his thinking. First, he attempted to extend the study of underdevelopment to areas outside Latin America in the hope of overcoming the limitations of dependence and finding a solution to the problem of underdevelopment. He acknowledged the contributions of Fernando Henrique Cardoso, Theotonio dos Santos, Osvaldo Sunkel, and others to the advancement of dependency theory, and he sought to apply the new ideas not only to the world outside Latin America but to an analysis of the dynamics of the world capitalist system as a whole.[78] Giovanni Arrighi had criticized Frank's effort to write a theoretical statement on dependency throughout the underdeveloped world, and Frank acknowledged his criticism: "Arrighi argued, it is the 'internal mode of production' that determines the 'external exchange relations,' and not vice versa, as I had maintained for the underdeveloped areas (circulation determining production in the periphery of the capitalist system, as Ruy Mauro Marini would later formulate it in 'dialectics of dependence' . . .)" (Frank 1978b, 14). The criticism of Samir Amin was also influential, according to Frank. Amin had charged that Frank neglected the world outside Latin America and had ignored the historical stages in the development of capitalism, and therefore Frank had turned to an analysis of the capitalist system on an integrated world scale. Influenced by Arghiri Emmanuel's *Unequal Exchange* (1972) and Amin's *Accumulation on a World Scale* (1974a), Frank emphasized international exchange. Although Frank seems to have influenced the world systems theory of Immanuel Wallerstein, he now was following in the latter's path.[79]

Several writings reflect the influence of Wallerstein upon Frank. His *Mexican Agriculture, 1521–1630* (1979) apparently was an attempt to respond to Arrighi's criticism, yet Frank also acknowledged the involvement of Wallerstein and his Fernand Braudel Center in the decision to publish.[80] Frank's *World Accumulation, 1492–1789* (1978b) focused on the historical evolution of capitalist accumulation in Western Europe. In the first volume of *Capital*, Marx had dated modern capitalism to the rapid expansion of commere and markets on a world level in the sixteenth century, a suggestion that was incorporated by Wallerstein in his *Modern World-System* (1974a, 1980) and argued by Frank in his study of world accumulation. Frank envisaged Europe as a superexploiter and expropriator of world wealth; the result was a dominant world economy and a dependent periphery. Another volume, *Dependent*

Accumulation and Underdevelopment (1978a), ambitiously attempted to explain why Europe, North America, and Australia developed while Africa, Asia, and Latin America remained underdeveloped; in examining three major periods of world capitalist development (mercantile, 1500–1770; industrial, 1770–1870; imperialist, since 1870), Frank attributes this regional differentiation to the consequences of world capital accumulation. These themes are carried on in subsequent works by Frank on the world economic crisis and crisis in the Third World.[81] Frank examined what he called the new economic and political crisis in the world, "centered on a new crisis of overaccumulation of capital in the capitalist West, and on the consequent transformation of its relations with the socialist East and the underdeveloped South" (Frank 1981b, ix).

My discussion has hinted at the criticism of Frank's thought on underdevelopment, and it is appropriate to identify and summarize some of the major concerns. In an early review of Frank's writing on capitalist underdevelopment, James Petras emphasized Frank's positive contributions: "It does not locate the causes and nature of underdevelopment in immediate events and policies . . . but from a dissection and analysis of the historical process. . . . Frank's most important contribution, however, is his brilliant critique of the myth of the Latin American feudal past" (Petras 1967, 50–51). Petras also indicated that Frank had provided little discussion of imperialism or of class structure. In probably the most celebrated criticism of Frank, Ernesto Laclau (1971) argued that Frank departed from Marxist theory by defining capitalism and feudalism as social systems governed by relationships of exchange rather than by modes of production and, further, that his approach made difficult any consistent analysis of the transition between feudalism and capitalism.

Two other assessments of Frank can help in an understanding of the weaknesses in his work. David Booth referred to early influences upon Frank: his training as an economist at the University of Chicago,[82] the work of the Economic Commission for Latin America in questioning traditional approaches to development based on association with foreign capital, and the Cuban Revolution. "Up to a point it makes sense to regard Frank as a radical critic of ECLA who was led by the force of his own argument to adopt anti-capitalist and ultimately Marxist positions. . . . without Fidel Castro, André Gunder Frank would not have been possible" (Booth 1975, 64). Booth continued with significant criticisms, including emphasis on external dependence despite Frank's insistence of the need to define underdevelopment in terms of classes and the absence of discussion of the links between modes of production within a single national or international economic system. In another critique, Aiden Foster-Carter contended that Frank operated with a different, and erroneous, problematic from that of Marx and Lenin; nevertheless, "Even if André Gunder Frank were as hopelessly wrong as many of his numerous assailants from all sides have maintained he is, there still remains the question as to why he is so important" (Foster-Carter 1976, 168). He answered this question by reference to Thomas Kuhn's thesis on paradigms: Frank had advanced an alternative paradigm to traditional diffusionist theories on development.

> Frank's great merit is to have, at a certain place and time, stated the new paradigm with such brute force that no one could possibly confuse it with anything else. Historically, this was perhaps necessary: later—in fact immediately—the critiques began, and it was discovered that Baran or the Latin American "structuralist" school had said it all before (to the extent that this is true, Frank never denied it), and that Frank's formulations are extremely crude: he sees capitalism everywhere, because he doesn't distinguish a mode of production from a social formation, and he wrongly assumes that exchange relations dominate production and that metropolis-satellite structures come before classes, and so on and so on. . . . What is in danger of being forgotten is that it was only because of Frank that we can now supersede him! [Foster-Carter 1976, 175–176]

The later work of Frank, of course, is also not without its critics. His historical account of world accumulation was subject to the scrutiny of Quentin Skinner, who referred to Frank's "inflexible theory of economic determinism" (Skinner 1979, 15) and offered three main objections. One was that "Frank adopts the old-fashioned view that the price revolution of the sixteenth century was primarily caused by imported bullion" when, in fact, "the mines at Potosí were not exploited on a large scale until the 1560s." Second, Frank assumed the existence of "a single global crisis" during the seventeenth century, but it is difficult to conceive of a global crisis at a time when China and Japan were so isolated. Finally, Frank's "emphasis on the role of international trade in explaining England's 'take-off' into sustained economic growth" was "implausible" (Skinner 1979, 15).

John Taylor attacked Frank on other grounds, for example, that the concept of economic surplus, which Frank drew from Baran's work, "precludes any rigorous analysis of the structure, reproduction and development of modes of production: hence it cannot provide an adequate basis for analysing either the development of capitalist penetration of non-capitalist modes, or the existence of different forms of this penetration." Taylor also believed that Frank tended to reduce explanations of social structure to a form of economic determinism, for example, in the thesis on underdevelopment where "crucial phenomena . . . remain unexplained"; "the basis is also laid here for a concomitant social reductionism"; and "the sociology of underdevelopment uses a unilinear social determinism" (Taylor 1979, 85, 91, 95, 96).

Anthony Brewer offered similar criticism:

> His normal procedure is to make brief, sloganistic assertions, and then to justify and expand on these by giving a series of historical examples, frequently quoting at length from other writers or from original sources. The problem with this style of argument is that it leaves no room for systematic theoretical exposition. . . . In addition, crucial terms (development, underdevelopment, metropolis, satellite, capitalism, and so on) are never explicitly defined. . . . It seems to me that Frank often allows these terms to have a spectrum of meanings rather than a single precisely defined sense, blurring the logic of some of his most important assertions. [Brewer 1980, 164–165]

Brewer expressed concern about Frank's "chain" of relationships between metropoles and satellites and called this a static system of redistribution in contrast to the view of classical Marxists such as Lenin and Bukharin, who argued that imperialism was part of a process of the internationalization of capitalism. As to Frank's emphasis on extraction of surplus from the satellite by the metropolis as an explanation for underdevelopment, Taylor insisted that analysis must focus on the use of surplus, for example, by merchant or multinational capital (Brewer 1980, 173–177).

Although Brewer, Taylor, and Booth have continued to dissect Frank's work, they are not afraid to recognize his important contributions. Not only has Frank challenged old thinking and stimulated new questions and research endeavors, he has emphasized capitalist underdevelopment and drawn attention to the need to analyze it in the context of a world system. This emphasis, in turn, has challenged radical scholars to evaluate his ideas in terms of classical and revised conceptions of Marxian theory. Nearly all the critics, and Frank himself, would agree that it is time to use these debates and assessments as a basis for moving into new areas of thinking about underdevelopment and development.

While Frank concentrated his attention on capitalist development of underdevelopment in Latin America, Walter Rodney focused on the historical experience of Africa in his widely read work, *How Europe Underdeveloped Africa* (1972).[83] Rodney began with a definition of development: "At the level of the individual, it implies increased skill and capacity, greater freedom, creativity, self-discipline, responsibility and material well-being" (Rodney 1972, 9). He believed that society develops economically as its members increase their collective capacity for dealing with the environment. In the struggle to exploit the resources of nature, specialization and division of labor result in more production and a better material life for some, but not all, members of society. Historical development has been a process of evolution through modes of production. All societies have experienced development, but the rate of development has been uneven from area to area. All phases of development, however, are temporary and transient and eventually must give way to some new social formation. Imperialism, for example, is a phase of capitalist development and has permitted the extension of capitalism to many parts of the world, while socialism has advanced on the weakest flanks of imperialism, especially in dependent areas where nationalism and a desire for independence were aroused among colonized peoples and where goals of production turned from money toward satisfaction of human needs. Thus underdevelopment is not the absence of development but is tied to the idea that development has been uneven. Some societies have advanced more by producing more and becoming more wealthy. Additionally, there has been the exploitation by one society of another—the consequence of colonialism, capitalism, and imperialism.

Rodney acknowledged the pejorative connotations of the term "underdevelopment," but dismissed efforts to replace it with the term "developing" because the latter implies that the countries of Africa, Asia, and Latin America can escape from their backward conditions and exploitation. "This certainly is not true, and many underdeveloped countries in Africa and elsewhere are becoming more underdeveloped in comparison with the world's great powers, because their exploitation by the metropoles is being intensified in new ways." Rodney also argued that the United States actually is the most underdeveloped country because it "practices external oppression on a massive scale, while internally there is a blend of exploitation, brutality, and psychiatric disorder" (Rodney 1972, 22).

Frank emphasizes that capital development and underdevelopment have characterized the world since the Middle Ages; societies may once have been undeveloped, but their underdevelopment was a direct result of capitalism. In contrast, Rodney stresses development, first in terms of individual needs and the prospects of society resolving its problems on a collective level, but he also identifies stages of development in the European experience (communalism, slavery, feudalism, capitalism, socialism). His emphasis on division of labor allows for a focus on class struggle through this history. The thesis that all societies will experience some development, even though it may be uneven, suggests that there will be a progressive evolution through capitalism to socialism. Both Rodney and Frank see underdevelopment as a consequence of capitalist exploitation. Both divide the world into metropoles and satellites and accept the premise that the underdeveloped countries are dependencies of the metropolitan capitalist economies. Both have little to say about strategies to overcome the condition of backwardness; they assume that the contradictions in the world capitalist system will produce struggles between ruling and exploited classes and that, eventually, socialism will emerge.

World Systems Theory: Immanuel Wallerstein

A sociologist by training, Immanuel Wallerstein was born in 1930, received his doctorate from Columbia University, and has taught at Columbia, McGill, and more recently at State University of New York, Binghamton. He first became prominent as a scholar on Africa (Wallerstein 1961, 1967)[84] and later turned his attention to an interpretative historical overview of the origins and evolution of the world capitalist system. In this enterprise, he was especially influenced by the methodology of the French historian Fernand Braudel. Braudel had participated in the prestigious French journal, *Annales,* and was well known for his work, *Civilisation matérielle, économie et capitalisme* (1979), which deals with the history of the world from the fifteenth to the nineteenth centuries.[85] At Binghamton, Wallerstein established the Fernand Braudel Center for the Study of Economies, Historical Systems, and Civilizations and the journal *Review,* which first appeared in 1977. One of its early issues examined the impact of the *Annales* school on the social sciences;[86] other issues were devoted to cycles and trends of the world system, the incorporation of southern Africa into the world eocnomy, and Chicano labor and unequal development.[87] Wallerstein was successful in aggregating at the center Marxist scholars with international reputations, such as Perry Anderson and Giovanni Arrighi. Research working groups were active on such topics as cyclical rhythms and secular trends of the capitalist world economy, households, labor force formation, the world economy, and the global labor market.[88] Wallerstein also was editor of the series Political Economy of the World System Annuals.[89]

Wallerstein's early essays set forth the essential concepts for the study of the world capitalist system.[90] Wallerstein defined world system "as a unit with a single division of labor and multiple cultural systems"

(1974b, 390). Two types of world systems are evident in history: world empires or the great civilizations of premodern times—such as those of China, Egypt, and Rome—and world economies dominated by nation-states and their colonial networks—exemplified by Great Britain and France. Wallerstein was especially concerned with the transition from feudalism to capitalism, and after reviewing the various positions, he tended to support André Gunder Frank and Paul Sweezy, who, while perhaps not faithfully following the arguments of Marx, nevertheless captured "an understanding of what actually happened" (Wallerstein 1974b, 393; see also 1976).

Looking to the experience of Europe, Wallerstein identified a core area in northwestern Europe, where there was highly skilled labor in agricultural production; a periphery in Eastern Europe and the Western Hemisphere, where there were exports of grains, cotton, sugar, and so on, and slavery or coerced cash-crop labor was predominant; and a semiperiphery in Mediterranean Europe, where there was agricultural sharecropping. Core, semiperiphery, and periphery thus represented three paths of national development in sixteenth-century Europe. Some areas came to be dependent on other areas as the core states emerged relatively strong under an absolute monarchy and a patrimonial state bureaucracy, whereas in the periphery there was no strong state (Wallerstein 1972, 96). Within these three categories, Wallerstein attempted to analyze three elements related to the formation of classes: a single market, state structures that distort the capitalist market, and the appropriation of surplus labor (Wallerstein 1975). He concluded that "the fundamental political reality of that world-economy is a class struggle which however takes constantly changing forms: overt class consciousness versus ethno-national consciousness, classes within nations versus classes across nations" (Wallerstein 1975, 375).

These themes pervade his multivolume work on the modern world system (1974a, 1980), which focuses on capitalist agriculture and the origins of the European economy in the sixteenth century and then turns to mercantilism and the consolidation of Europe in the seventeenth and early eighteenth centuries. In this work, Wallerstein examined the breakup of feudalism, the rise of the centralized state bureaucracies, and the social organization of agriculture. He argued that the crisis of feudalism was represented by "a conjuncture of secular trends, an immediate cyclical crisis, and climatological decline" (Wallerstein 1974a, 37), the consequence of which was the formation of the capitalist world economy as a new form of surplus appropriation. Essential to this development were an expansion of the geographical frontiers of Europe, the control over different products from different regions, and the formation of strong state apparatuses. He summarized his argument:

"As of 1450, the stage was set in Europe but not elsewhere for the creation of a capitalist world-economy. This system was based on two key institutions, a world-wide division of labor and bureaucratic state machineries in certain areas" (Wallerstein 1974a, 63). He argued that after 1600, "although the boundaries of the world-economy remained largely the same . . . there was a difference . . . regarding the allocation of resources, economic roles, and wealth and poverty and location of wage employment and industrial enterprise (Wallerstein 1980, 8).

Brewer, comparing the thought of Wallerstein with that of Frank, found that both related capitalism to a network of exchange relations on a world scale in which surplus tends to be transferred from periphery to core. Both emphasized the world economy as a whole rather than its particular parts and internal structure. Both felt that the organization of production on the local or national level was secondary to that on the international level. Both argued that development and underdevelopment were opposite sides of the same phenomenon, each being the result of the other. Although he felt that the two writers had contributed significantly in their insistence on analysis of underdevelopment in terms of a world system, he found fault with their work: "There is little connection between their grandiose general statements and their (often very illuminating) discussion of particular historical cases. What is lacking is real theory. I have suggested that theories based on the Marxist analysis of relations of production could fill this gap" (Brewer 1980, 181).

Chase-Dunn and Rubinson (1977) offered a useful synthesis of Wallerstein's description of the emergence of the world system and some of its features and went on to describe the processes that reproduce the world system, with attention to the division of labor between the core and the periphery. Peter Worsley objected to Wallerstein's assumption that capitalism is a system in which production is for exchange, dependent on the market rather than on the way commodities are produced. Further, the model of world capitalism is "over-deterministic," and it emphasizes how ruling classes manipulate the system, while paying scant attention to the resistance to their domination (Worsley 1980, 304–305).

Verl F. Hunt challenged Wallerstein's assertion that trade determines the pattern of economic development throughout capitalist Europe. In particular, he focused on the origins and evolution of feudalism in Eastern Europe. He objected to the characterization of Eastern Europe as capitalist and the tying together of Eastern and Western Europe into a single system.

> The economic systems of Eastern and Western Europe are simply labeled capitalist—defined as the relations between owners of output

and the market. Consequently, Wallerstein's use of the term "mode of production" does not convey the particular forces and technical relations of economic production, which, when combined with social relationships, together form the basis of societal formations. Wallerstein is unfortunately insensitive to the diverse social totalities prevailing in 16th-century Europe. [Hunt 1978, 60]

Hunt argued that during the transition period of European history there emerged an uneven mixture of feudal and capitalist elements. Furthermore, the pattern of development differed substantially in Eastern and Western Europe. In the West, an urban bourgeoisie formed, leading to an increase in commodity production and the rise of manufacturing capital; thus primitive accumulation and the gradual dissolution of feudal ties to the countryside began. In the East, a mixture of feudal and capitalist structures evolved, but it was accompanied by absolutism as a mechanism for "imposing servitude on the communal poor in a social landscape devoid of urban resistance" (Hunt 1978, 61).

A similar criticism was made by C. H. George: "Wallerstein's problem begins with his version of feudalism, which reflects distressing ignorance of the sources and much of the major scholarship, particularly that of the English variety essential to his thesis." George attacked Wallerstein for his "misreading of texts" and argued that his thesis rests on "an encyclopedia of misinformation" (George 1980, 87). He suggested that there is "a great deal more of Hegel in Wallerstein than there is of Marx" and that the "leitmotiv of his book is an idealized construction of the orgins of the modern world" (George 1980, 89).

Robert Brenner pointed to the tendency of Wallerstein, following in the path of Paul Sweezy, to equate capitalism with a division of labor based on trade, an assumption Brenner believed was drawn from the work of Adam Smith. Although Wallerstein differed from Smith in his concern for class, he also attempted to assimilate new class relations of production with commercial development. Brenner criticized Wallerstein for implying that the transition from feudalism to capitalism was a smooth and linear process, in fact involving no transition at all: "In Wallerstein's *The Modern World System*, the Smithian theory embedded in Sweezy's analysis of the transition from feudalism to capitalism is made entirely explicit, and carried to its logical conclusion" (Brenner 1977, 53). Failing to focus "on the productivity of labour as the essence and key to economic development," he argued, Wallerstein "did not see the degree to which patterns of development or underdevelopment for an entire epoch might hinge upon the outcome of specific processes of class formation, of class struggle" (Brenner 1977, 91).

Underdevelopment and Unequal Development: Amin and Emmanuel

Born in 1931 in Egypt, Samir Amin received his doctorate in economics in Paris. He has been a professor of economics at the universities of Dakar, Poitiers, and Paris and served as director of the African Institute for Economic Development and Planning in Dakar. He is the author of many popular books on development and underdevelopment, among them *Accumulation on a World Scale* (1974a), *Unequal Development* (1976b), *Imperialism and Unequal Development* (1977, 1976a), *The Law of Value and Historical Materialism* (1978b), and *Class and Nation* (1980). Amin also has published important works on the Middle East and Africa, including *Neo-Colonialism in West Africa* (1973), *The Maghreb in the Modern World: Algeria, Tunisia, Morocco* (1970), and *The Arab Nation* (1978a).[91]

In his *Accumulation on a World Scale*, he systematically attacked mainstream writing on political economy and development, synthesized the ideas and concepts of Marx and other Marxists, and offered a theory of underdevelopment. His theory departed from the assumption that the world comprises developed and undeveloped countries, some of which are capitalist and others socialist, all integrated into a commercial and financial network on a world scale: "There are not two world markets, one capitalist and the other socialist, but only one, the capitalist world market, in which Eastern Europe marginally participates" (Amin 1974a, 1:4). He considered accumulation "an essential inner law of the capitalist mode of production and doubtless also of the socialist mode of production, but . . . not an inner law of the functioning of precapitalist modes of production" (Amin 1974a, 1:2). He discussed primitive accumulation in the breakdown of precapitalist modes and emphasized "the transfers of value" that take place as the capitalist mode of production enters into relations with the precapitalist modes.

Amin went on to characterize underdevelopment in terms of unevenness of productivity, disarticulation of the economy, and domination from the outside. Uneven levels of productivity are found everywhere, even in advanced countries where progress is usually associated with new industries. Disarticulation of the economy is attributable to the lack of communication between different sectors of the economy. Domination from the outside is the consequence of dependence. External dependence is characterized by a few large-scale enterprises, usually foreign, that rely on large international businesses and centers outside the underdeveloped country. Thus external dependence appears with external trade, involving exports of primary products for imports of goods manufactured abroad. This commercial dependence is often accompanied by increasing financial dependence upon investments of foreign capital that result in an outflow of profits and a return of capital to the advanced countries. These conditions necessitate a rapid growth of exports so as to offset the accelerating growth of imports brought about by urbanization and the insufficient local production of food; rapid increases in administrative expenses in proportion to the needs of the local economy; unequal income distribution, resulting in consumption by the privileged strata; and inadequate industrialization, necessitating imports of capital goods. Amin summarized the impact of such conditions on development and underdevelopment: "Whereas at the center, growth *is* development—that is, it has an integrating effect—in the periphery growth *is not* development, for its effect is to disarticulate. Strictly speaking, growth in the periphery, based on integration into the world market, is *development of underdevelopment* (Amin 1974a, 1:18–19).

Given this perspective, and its similarity to that of Frank, Amin proceeded to construct a theory of the international division of labor and of the accumulation of capital on a world scale. He warned against misunderstanding: "Confusion between independent precapitalist economies and societies . . . and economies and societies integrated into the dominant capitalist world through the historical fact of colonial subjection . . . is what lies behind the mistaken ideas of the theory of underdevelopment" (Amin 1974a, 1:20). The theory of accumulation on a world scale, he argued, involves relations between the center and the periphery. Basing his theory on Marxist concepts, including the mode of production and capitalist formations, Amin acknowledged the contribution of Lenin to analysis of the transformation at the center and the formation of monopolies, but he insisted that formations in the periphery had not been examined carefully. Baran and Sweezy had updated the work of Lenin, but they did not show the connections between transformations in the center and those in the periphery. With this perspective, it would be possible to sweep away the false concepts of underdevelopment and Third World and replace them with the concept of "capitalist formations on the periphery" (Amin 1974a, 1:23).

Amin related this concept to class on national and international levels. He believed that focus on mode of production leads to attention to "national capitalisms" and the relationship of a bourgeoisie and a proletariat of each country. This emphasis on mode of production must be replaced by attention to the system of capitalist formations on a world scale.

> The social contradictions characteristic of capitalism are thus on a world scale, that is, the contradiction is not between the bourgeoisie

> and the proletariat of each country considered in isolation, but between the world bourgeoisie and the world proletariat. This world bourgeoisie and this world proletariat exist in a context not of the capitalist mode of production but of the system of capitalist formations—which . . . means the formations at the center and the formations in the periphery. [Amin 1974a, 1:24]

In his discussion of development in the periphery, Amin argued that a first step was the creation of a homogeneous national economy, which could be accomplished by shifting workers with low levels of productivity to areas of high productivity and from agriculture to industry. In addition, centers or poles of development could be deliberately established, with integrated industrial groups promoting "autocentric" or autonomous activity. Finally, there would be changes in the structure of foreign trade and distribution of income and financing to stimulate development.

Amin addressed the question of whether a socialist world is possible. His solution of autocentric national structures, he felt, poses a contradiction to the traditional way capitalism operates, whereas socialism, in order to be effective, would integrate the world on the basis of equality. But the task of building socialism would be difficult. Socialism cannot involve a division of labor based on the market; specialization would be on equitable terms until nations withered away. The transition to socialism would involve the seeking of new forms to erode the vestiges of precapitalist traditions and to confront the "limited, peripheral, dependent . . . road of the limited capitalist development of today" (Amin 1974a, 1:34).

The second of Amin's major works, *Unequal Development*, focuses on unequal development and the social formations of peripheral capitalism. The first of five parts examines the precapitalist modes of production: the communal mode, characterized by organization of labor on both individual and collective bases, an absence of exchange, and distribution of the product within the collectivity in accordance with rules associated with kinship organization; the tribute-paying mode, represented by division between the peasantry and the ruling class; the feudal mode, in which the separation between lords of the land and the serf-tenants prevails; and the slave-owning mode, in which the workers are slaves. According to Amin, societies comprise "formations" in which modes and relations of production are combined. Precapitalist social formations are characterized by the dominance of the communal or the tribute-paying mode of production, the existence of simple commodity relations, and a pattern of trade relations based on long distance.

The second part focused on the capitalist mode of production and its three defining features: It takes the form of commodities, labor itself becomes a commodity, and the means of production become commodities appropriated by a ruling class. Private ownership of the means of production at first characterizes the capitalist mode, but at a certain stage, state ownership takes the place of private ownership by social groups on a national scale. Amin analyzed these aspects in the light of what he called autocentric accumulation. He also related accumulation to international trade patterns and monetary flows.

A third part delves into international trade and specialization, then turns to the theory of unequal exchange advocated by Arghiri Emmanuel, and concludes with an exposition of dependency in the periphery, which he described as being related to the need of central capitalism for cheap labor in the periphery. At an early stage, the periphery emphasizes exports of raw materials to the center, thus restricting and distorting the local market and allowing expansion of the market at the center with the periphery "serving only a marginal, subordinate, and limited function" (Amin 1976b, 193). In a later stage, an internal market does appear; it favors demand for luxury goods rather than mass consumer goods.

> If *all* the capital invested in the exporting sector were foreign, and if *all* the profits of this capital were repatriated to the center, the internal market would consist entirely of a demand for mass consumer goods, as restricted as the reward of labor is low. But some of this capital is local. Furthermore, the methods employed so as to ensure that the reward of labor is low are based on strengthening those local parasitic social groups which function as transmission belts: latifundia-owners, kulaks, comprador trading bourgeoisie, state bureaucracy, etc. The internal market will thus be based mainly upon the demand of these social groups for luxury products. [Amin 1976b, 193]

Amin called this link between the exporting sector and luxury consumption "a specific articulation . . . characteristic of this dependent, peripheral model of accumulation and economic development" (Amin 1976b, 193). He believed that industrialization occurs at the end of the process, corresponding to an advanced state of development in the center, that is, the production of consumer goods. At this stage, the production of luxury goods begins to take the place of imports and subsistence agriculture stagnates, but because production for mass consumption cannot occur, most of the population remains impoverished and "marginalized." Unevenness of development, which is the consequence of unequal exchange on a world scale, is evident with this impoverishment of the masses and the integration of a wealthy minority into the world system. Thus class struggle must be examined on a world scale: "It means that the bourgeoisie of the center, the only one that exists on the scale of the world system, exploits the proletariat everywhere, at the center and at the periphery, but that it exploits the proletariat of the periphery even more brutally" (Amin 1976b, 196).

A fourth part of this study looks at the origins of capitalist development of underdevelopment. Here Amin advanced nine theses on the transition to peripheral capitalism that show the unevenness of development in the periphery and then went on to examine the contemporary social formations of the periphery: American, Arab, Asian, and African. He found that these peripheral social formations are characterized by a predominance of agrarian capital in the national sector, the generation of a local or merchant bourgeoisie in the path of the dominant foreign capital, and a tendency toward formation of a bureaucracy (see Amin 1976–1977).

Amin concluded with the question of how the transition to capitalism can be achieved. The choice is either dependent or auto-centric development in the periphery, and given the unevenness of development, "the periphery cannot just overtake the capitalist model; it is obliged to surpass it." Amin argued that the transition on a world scale begins with the liberation of the periphery and a local model of accumulation. "A development that is not merely development of underdevelopment will therefore be both national, popular-democratic, and socialist, by virtue of the world project of which it forms part" (Amin 1976b, 383).

Chris Chase-Dunn acknowledged that *Unequal Development* is "an ambitious and largely successful attempt to apply Marx's accumulation model of capitalist development to the world economy as a whole." He felt that the work suffers, however, from "lack of attention to the state, the process of state formation, and the state system" (Chase-Dunn 1978b, 85; see also 1978a). Alan Sica was awed by the breadth and knowledge necessary to contend with Amin: "Amin is truly in a class by himself, which probably ensures that criticism will be leveled only at those small portions of his work which irritate various specialists" (Sica 1978, 730). Martin Bronfenbrenner (1978) believed that Amin's writings on accumulation and unequal development were successful efforts to update and reconstruct Lenin's theory of imperialism and Luxemburg's theory of capital accumulation (also see Sau 1975). Ira Gerstein complained that Amin "never discusses relations of production" and felt that Amin's treatment of class struggle is "obscure" and that of the transition to socialism "somewhat ambiguous."

However, the inadequacies of Amin's analysis, particularly his emphasis on the market with the resultant tendency toward dualism, masking the class struggle, and ignoring the relations of production, lead him to a questionable world class analysis. . . . Thus the struggle for socialism proceeds in combination and merger with a struggle for national liberation in the periphery, conceptualized as a struggle for independent national *development*, in which the national bourgeoisie will then play an important role. . . . In his work, however, Amin does not emphasize the class struggle. Rather, he is concerned with technical prescriptions that would presumably be useful to the national bourgeoisie in its struggle for "independent development." [Gerstein 1977, 15]

Although recognizing some of these shortcomings, Morten Ougaard emphasized that the appeal of Amin's analysis relates to his attention to reproduction structures. Reproduction of capitalism is less a possibility in the periphery than the center because "peripheral societies lack the important linkage between production of consumer-goods and production of producer-goods" and such weakness "gives the peripheral reproduction structure a far less dynamic character than the reproduction structure of center-capitalism," resulting in the blocking of development in the periphery (Ougaard 1982–1983, 387). Anthony Brewer, after showing how Amin took his analysis of international prices from Emmanuel and added his own discussion of unequal specialization, concluded that "together these theories amount to the first serious analysis of international trade in the Marxist tradition" (Brewer 1980, 236). Brewer identified the relationship between the thought of Amin and that of Baran and some dependency theorists, but he acknowledged that little was drawn from Frank with the exception of the idea of development of underdevelopment. He concluded with a sober assessment of Amin.

His is the only serious attempt to tackle what is surely the central problem, that of analysing accumulation on a world scale, a dynamic process involving social formations of very divergent structures linked into a single world capitalist economy. In the process, he tried to link together a range of subjects that had previously been studied in virtual isolation from each other: modes of production, class structure in the periphery, the pattern of international trade and specialisation, the formation of international prices, the (economic) problems of national development in the periphery, the periodisation of capitalist development, and so on. To pose the problem is often the most important step. [Brewer 1980, 257]

The contribution of Arghiri Emmanuel on these questions is embodied principally in his *Unequal Exchange* (1972), which, departing from the analysis in the third volume of Marx's *Capital*, attempts to relate what Emmanuel called "the imperialism of trade" to the exploitation of poor nations and peoples. An understanding of this work necessitates a careful reading of *Capital* itself and familiarity with the debate on the labor theory of value. Rather than attempt to work through the details, I shall only quote at some length from Charles Bettelheim's critique of Emmanuel's work.

Bettelheim argues that Emmanuel makes a substantial contribution in developing a radical criticism of David Ricardo's thesis on comparative costs and the natural advantages of countries participating in exchange, helping to expose the myth that the capitalist international division of labor has advantages not only for the wealthy countries but also for the poor ones. Emmanuel showed that through time, the poorer countries tend to become poorer and the richer ones, richer. However, he saw a weakness in Emmanuel's analysis in that it "isolates the 'moment of exchange,' that is, . . . fails to situate it within the field of production relations and productive forces and to integrate it in the structure of capitalism as a world system. Thus, something is ascribed to 'exchange conditions' that is really an effect of the structure of the capitalist system on the world scale" (Bettelheim, in Emmanuel 1972, 311).

Bettelheim attacked Emmanuel's formulation as portraying a situation in which capitalist production relations have penetrated a homogeneous world economy whose units are distinguished by differences of specialization in the international division of labor and by unequal wage levels. This portrayal obscures the exploitation of the working people everywhere and the exploitation of some classes by others. Bettelheim felt that the model set forth by Emmanuel did not deal with unequal relations: "The theoretical construction he proposes to substitute for these dogmas does not enable us to grasp at the root the conditions for the expanded reproduction of *unequal relations* (and not merely of 'unequal exchange')." Consequently, Emmanuel has "mutilated" Marxist concepts, and his "problematic directs us toward illusory reformist solutions" (Emmanuel 1972, 315–316). The reformism is inherent in the implication that prices and wages can be manipulated to bring about a revolutionary transformation of production relations along with a development of productive forces that offers the possibility of eliminating poverty in the dominated countries. Bettelheim further argued that Emmanuel's position is "clearly irreconcilable with Marxism, since it consists in denying the existence of the class struggle in the industrialized countries" (Emmanuel 1972, 352).[92] Emmanuel thus found himself in the position of arguing with other specialists on underdevelopment who stressed the differences between wealthy and poor countries rather than between bourgeoisies and proletariats.[93]

In his rejoinder to Bettelheim, Emmanuel made it clear that he did not feel compelled to follow Marxist orthodoxy, particularly as related to the law of value. He argued that there can be no exchange value without private ownership. He stated he did not believe in absolute value, thus explaining a fundamental disagreement with Bettelheim. Bettelheim, however, referred to a deep difference between theoretical positions. Since Emmanuel emphasized "claims" rather than "laws" in what lies beyond political economy, Bettelheim felt that Emmanuel had not yet understood "the epistemological break that enabled Marx to found the doctrine of historical materialism and thus to replace political economy by a science of modes of production and social formations" (Emmanuel 1972, 345). Emmanuel, he believed, had assumed a "precritical" position, founded on the work of the early Marx and not on his later and mature writings. This precritical position "includes certain petty-bourgeois revolutionary movements. . . . This current rejects the leading role of the proletariat, substituting for the fundamental conflict recognized by Marxism, namely, that between bourgeoisie and proletariat, another conflict, namely that between 'advanced' countries and 'underdeveloped' ones, or between 'rich' and 'poor' countries" (Emmanuel 1972, 347).

6 / Old and New Perspectives in Retrospect

This study has examined two contemporary perspectives on development and underdevelopment, one emphasizing capitalism and reformism and the other, socialism and revolution. The concern with capitalist underdevelopment, especially in the less advanced countries, has also been related to attention to the world system. This final chapter has two objectives: to summarize the major findings and compare and contrast the various perspectives and to identify the principal criticisms of theories of development and underdevelopment.

I have identified interpretations that emphasize the positive consequences of capitalism as diffusionist and illustrated them with examples such as the emphasis on Western electoral democracy, nationalism, and linear growth toward modernization found in political science and political sociology. Although these approaches have been criticized for an ethnocentric bias and the unexamined assumption that Western technology and capital can be diffused so as to ensure development of the backward parts of the world, they continue to influence contemporary theory. In contrast, theories of underdevelopment usually stress the negative consequences of capitalism. A good portion of this volume is devoted to discussion and criticism of these theories. In particular, they have been assessed in the light of the solution to the problem they advocate or imply—reform or revolution, capitalist or socialist development.

My review has focused on the principal thinkers and their contributions to the literature on development and underdevelopment, and Table 1 offers a chronological summary of their ideas since the forties. The initial theory seemed to emanate from distinct origins, and there is little evidence to suggest that the various writers influenced each other. Although Raúl Prebisch and Sergio Bagú were Argentine intellectuals who wrote early about the distinction between center and periphery, they were influenced by different considerations—Prebisch by his training as an economist and experience in central banking and international financial operations, Bagú by his teaching and research as an economic historian. Bagú and Caio Prado Júnior both wrote about dependent economies under colonialism, but they were of different nationalities and apparently not influenced by each other. Silvio Frondizi

109

Table 1. Evolution of Ideas on Development and Underdevelopment in the Third World

Pioneering Efforts Prior to 1960	Decade of the Sixties	Decade of the Seventies
Center and periphery usage (1944: Bagú, Prebisch)	Developmental poles (Perroux, Andrade)	Associated dependent capitalist development (Cardoso)
Dependent economy in colonial society (1942: Prado Júnior; 1949: Bagú)	Attack on feudalism and national bourgeoisie (Prado, Vitale)	European underdevelopment of Africa (Rodney)
Contradiction of two imperialisms (1947: Frondizi)	Capitalist development of underdevelopment (Frank)	Subimperialism (Marini)
ECLA *desarrollista* approach (1948)	New dependency (Dos Santos)	Dependency, imperialism, and class struggle (Quijano)
Political economy of growth and backwardness (1957: Baran)	External dependency and regional planning as solution (Furtado)	Combined and uneven development (Mandel, Novack)
	Autonomous nationalist response as solution to North-South dichotomy (Sunkel)	World system theory (Wallerstein)
	Internal colonialism (González Casanova)	Unequal development (Amin)
	Structural dependency (Cardoso and Faletto)	Unequal exchange (Emmanuel)
	Monopoly capital (Baran and Sweezy)	Mode of production (Laclau, Taylor)
		Internationalization of capital (Palloix)
		Imperialism as impetus for capitalism (Warren)
		Late capitalism (Mandel)

did not cite these writers in his own early assessment of imperialism and dependent economies and was more influenced by classical Marxist thought.

The contemporary writers of the sixties and seventies frequently referred to Prebisch and sometimes to Bagu and Prado. André Gunder Frank acknowledged his indebtedness to Baran. Writers like Celso Furtado and Osvaldo Sunkel seldom mentioned the classical thinkers— Marx, Lenin, and Trotsky—whose ideas are relevant today. Theotonio dos Santos and Ruy Mauro Marini often referred to these earlier writers, while Fernando Henrique Cardoso emphasized his updating of Lenin's theory of imperialism and Aníbal Quijano moved toward a class analysis in a Marxist tradition. Recent writers like Amin, Emmanuel, Mandel, and Warren were very explicit in relating their ideas to classical thought. However, the writing of all these thinkers is generally considered revisionist, that is, comprising modification and extension of the earlier Marxism.

Since so many lines of thinking have emanated from the literature, a synthesis showing similarities and differences may be helpful. Table 2 provides an impressionistic sketch of reformist, nationalist, and capitalist views, and Table 3 gives a comparison of revolutionary and socialist views.

Nationalism and concern about imperialism since the Second World War have led many theorists to espouse the position that Third World countries might be able to transform themselves through an expanding capitalism that develops autonomously. The assumption was that because the United States had developed autonomously along a capitalist path, underdeveloped nations might likewise do so. Finding a way to ensure that development was autonomous was the concern of Raúl Prebisch, who modified some of his neoclassical economic understanding in an effort to cope with underdevelopment in Latin America. François Perroux and followers like Manuel Correia de Andrade offered a scheme that would allow for both capitalist autonomy and multinational investment. Celso Furtado looked to nationalist planning under the capitalist state, and Osvaldo Sunkel took a similar position. Pablo González Casanova and Fernando Henrique Cardoso recognized the limitations of capitalist development influenced by imperialism, but they also considered capitalism progressive.

Prebisch was one of the first to turn attention from the advanced capitalist nations and to divide the world into a center and periphery, a structural approach that has been followed by most of the thinkers under consideration. This structuralism is evident in the writing of Furtado, Sunkel, and Cardoso and implied in the approach of Perroux and Andrade. Although with the latter the distinction is somewhat

Table 2. Reformist, Nationalist, and Capitalist Views on Development and Underdevelopment

	ECLA School (Prebisch)	Poles of Developmentalists (Perroux, Andrade)	ECLA Revisionists (Sunkel, Furtado, Cardoso)	Internal Colonialists (González Casanova)
Uses structural approach: Center and periphery	x	x	x	x
Sees dependency as cause of deformation and stagnation	x	x	x	x
Stresses impact of market and relations of exchange rather than production	x	x	x	x
Assumes capitalism as dominant in periphery since colonial period	?	?	?	
Emphasizes class analysis				
Opposes imperialism			x	x
Favors socialism			?	x
Advocates revolutionary path				?
Links national bourgeoisie to imperialism			?	
Strongly criticizes bourgeois-democratic revolution				

Table 3. Revolutionary and Socialist Views on Development and Underdevelopment

	Pioneer Thinkers (Frondizi, Bagú, Prado)	New dependentistas (Dos Santos, Marini, Quijano)	Trotskyists (Vitale, Novack, Mandel)	Underdevelopmentalists (Baran, Frank)	Unequal Developmentalists (Amin, Emmanuel)	World System Theorists (Wallerstein, Frank)
Uses structural approach: Center and periphery	x	x	x	x	x	x
Sees dependency as cause of deformation and stagnation	x	x	x	x	x	x
Stresses impact of market and relations of exchange rather than production	x	x	x	x	x	x
Assumes capitalism as dominant in periphery since colonial period	x	x	x	x	x	x
Emphasizes class analysis	x	x	x	x		
Opposes imperialism	x	x	x	x	x	x
Favors socialism	x	x	x	x	x	x
Advocates revolutionary path	x	x	x	x	x	x
Links national bourgeoisie to imperialism	x	x	x	x	x	?
Strongly criticizes bourgeois-democratic revolution	x	x	x	x	x	?

blurred by their diffusionist solution, their proposal to establish poles of development in the backward periphery suggests that the model of center and periphery is relevant to their formulation. González Casanova simply substituted "metropolis" and "satellite" for "center" and "periphery."

Prebisch also emphasized the need to establish an infrastructure, impose tariffs on imported luxury and capital goods, and build industry to produce for national consumption. Furtado advocated a similar strategy. Although Prebisch was emphatic that his reforms would counter the underconsumption that had caused backwardness and underdevelopment, Sunkel, Furtado, and Cardoso attributed the difficulties of capitalist reproduction in the periphery to the limited consumption of the national bourgeoisie. Presumably, most of these writers believed that central planning and investment by the state are essential to industrialization. Only Perroux advocated multinational investment, but under a plan that he believed would ensure a national direction.

All the writers referred to dependency and underdevelopment in some form. For Prebisch, the internal contradictions of the periphery prevented the capitalist development that occurred in the center; the periphery lacked capital and was excluded from the exchange of goods that benefited the center. Dependency on the center was a condition of peripheral capitalism. Sunkel saw the nation-state as subordinate to the international capitalist system. Furtado related dependency and underdevelopment to hybrid structures incorporating capitalist and precapitalist features. González Casanova, with his conception of internal colonialism, stressed the relationships of metropolis to satellite within a nation; he saw dominant monopoly control over the marginal and outlying areas as resulting in deformation and exploitation. Cardoso suggested that some dependent situations in the periphery offered the possibility of progressive capitalism and growth rather than stagnancy.

Although most of these writers emphasized the consequences of market and trade, Furtado and González Casanova also focused attention on precapitalist social formations; Cardoso also mentioned various classes under capitalism. Reference to classes permitted an elementary class analysis, although emphasis on market patterns provoked criticism that their definition was not grounded in a class analysis. All three incorporated a conception of dualism. Cardoso wrote of a duality that permitted some local participation in production while large foreign corporations reorganized the international division of labor so as to include some dependent economies in their plans of investment. González Casanova separated the marginalized Indian masses from the bourgeois and working-class populations of the center in Mexico. Furtado's dualistic economy was based on a combination of precapitalist and capitalist features. González Casanova and Cardoso also examined the role of the national bourgeoisie, especially its prospects for fomenting development. At the same time, they took a socialist stance; their advocacy of capitalism assumed that capitalism was necessary en route to socialism. One might assume that Furtado and Sunkel agreed with this position, although a preference for socialism is more implicit than explicit in their writings.

At the same time that these reformist views were being formulated and debated, several prominent leftist writers were advocating a revolutionary course in the direction of socialism. These writers shared anti-imperialist sentiments but sought to combine their concern about external influences with analysis of the internal structural conditions of their respective countries. For most writers, this effort resulted in a clear identification of the national bourgeoisie with imperialism and a condemnation of the bourgeois-democratic revolution.

Caio Prado Júnior, for example, arrived at this position after the 1964 military coup in Brazil; previously he had followed the line of the Brazilian Communist party, which called for an alliance with the national bourgeoisie and advocacy of a progressive capitalism within a nationalist framework. Theotonio dos Santos had participated in the social fervor of the early sixties in Brazil, a period that had promised the possibility of the achievement of socialism through movements of mass mobilization, parliamentary democracy, and an ideology of nationalism and development, but he was disillusioned by the military takeover and what he described as the rise of fascism in many countries of Latin America. Aníbal Quijano wrote about nationalism and dependency in his early studies of Peru, and his attention to these themes clearly placed him in the school of writers interested in revising some of Marx's early formulations. Later he emphasized imperialism and an internal analysis of social classes in Peru. Ruy Mauro Marini described how capitalism in the periphery leads to subimperialism, and Sergio Bagú traced conditions of dependency to the colonial period of Latin American development. Silvio Frondizi analyzed the weakness of national capital in the face of monopoly capital and imperialism.

All these writers saw dependency as a cause of the deformation and stagnation that characterized underdevelopment in Latin America. All of them, like the reformist writers, employed a structural approach that separated the center of advanced capitalist nations from the periphery of less developed ones. All assumed that capitalism had dominated the periphery since the colonial period, and all except Marini stressed the impact of merchant capital and market considerations over that of capitalist production.

Frondizi examined differences between British commercial imperialism and U.S. industrial imperialism and exposed the weaknesses of the Argentine bourgeoisie in the face of both. Neither a strong state apparatus nor a national bourgeoisie could overcome this imperialism through a bourgeois-democratic revolution. Thus an underdeveloped country would tend to become more dependent on the capitalist centers of the world.

Bagú acknowledged only traces of feudalism in the early colonial period of Latin America, for the colonial economies, he believed, were subject to the foreign market; thus conditions of dependency, stagnation and deformation in particular, were evident as the colonies integrated themselves into the new capitalist cycle and the feudalism of the Iberian Peninsula was unable to reproduce itself abroad. Merchant capitalism, not feudalism, was the only possibility for Latin America.

Although some of his ideas changed dramatically after 1964, Prado's historical treatment consistently emphasized the commercial basis of the Brazilian economy in the productive activities of the large estate, monoculture, and slave labor. The externally oriented economy was based on the production of commodities for the international market and trade with Portugal. Prado demonstrated that these commodities served only international markets and that efforts to establish domestic manufacturing industries had failed. Further, Brazil suffered from cyclical development in which the fortunes of gold and sugar, then cotton, rubber, and coffee, rose and declined with international demand and supply. Whatever bourgeoisie prevailed in Brazil was tied to the outside world. Under such circumstances, there could be no hope for a national bourgeoisie, and only revolutionary struggle and national liberation could lead to a way out of the dilemma.

Dos Santos began with the assumption that imperialist centers dominated the world economy, and his identification of historical periods of dependency corresponded to the classification that other writers had offered for imperialism. He contrasted dominant with dependent nations but accepted the premise that the dependent ones could develop either positively or negatively as a consequence of the expansion and self-sustaining efforts of the dominant ones. Thus development could be seen in terms of unequal and combined development; that is, various modes of production (both precapitalist and capitalist) might be evident in the development of the peripheral nation. For the most part, Dos Santos focused on international commodity and capital markets, foreign exchange, and multinational corporations that contributed to what he termed "the new dependency" after the Second World War. He theorized that a system of dependent production reproduced itself in the periphery, leading to backwardness and superexploitation. Thus, in the face of imperialism and the multinationals, the industrial bourgeoisie in Brazil could not carry out its mission of development. The option of autonomous national development had failed for the industrial and petty bourgeoisies, but radical elements emanating from the nationalist movement of the early sixties offered the possibility of advancement through nationalist revolution and armed struggle.

Marini's thought also emerged from the popular movements of the early sixties that linked nationalism with Marxism in Brazil, and he partially identified with the theses of Frank and Dos Santos. He accepted the proposition that capitalism promoted underdevelopment in the periphery, but he focused attention on dependent capitalism that could not reproduce itself internally in Brazil but extended outside the national borders to penetrate the economies of weaker neighbors in a process he called subimperialism. Subimperialism, he argued, affected both national productivity and expansionist policy. On the national level, the bourgeoisie remained dependent on the U.S. monopolies, thus precluding the possibility of significant Brazilian development and ensuring a continued exploitation of the mass of workers. Given this situation, the proletariat might be able to lead the nation along a revolutionary course against the subimperialist bourgeoisie and imperialism itself. Focusing on relations of production, Marini thus differed from other thinkers who emphasized market and trade considerations.

Quijano offered an explicit classification of class categories, both in his early analysis of the failure of nationalism and national autonomous development in Peru and in his later examination of imperialism. Consequently, he was able to combine his focus on imperialism with his initial formulation of dependency. After the Second World War, he argued, imperialist expansion resulted in the denationalization of control over capital and closer bonds between the national and imperialist bourgeoisies. He believed that Peru had been affected by the uneven and combined character of its development, resulting in contradictions between capitalism and the remnants of precapitalism. He saw such contradictions as reflecting a loss of political power among the feudal-mercantile landowners and an increase of power among the new elements of the bourgeoisie. With this increase of power, the new bourgeoisie in Peru had aligned itself with the intermediate sectors and the proletariat. In countries where this bourgeoisie did not establish a hegemony, the military often intervened to control the apparatuses of the state.

Luis Vitale, George Novack, and Ernest Mandel understood development in much the same way as Dos Santos, Marini, and Quijano. In the first place, they all emphasized the dominance of capitalism in the peripheral economies. Vitale was particularly emphatic that the Spanish conquest was oriented to the exploitation and commercialization of precious metals and to a system of capitalist production thereafter. Feudal lords did not rule in Latin America, where there was a bourgeoisie dependent on the world market. The result of this dependency in both colonial and imperialist periods was backwardness and underdevelopment. Second, all these writers stressed the uneven and combined character of development, and third, they emphasized the dependent nature of the periphery and the problems of unequal exchange in the capitalist world economy. Finally, they focused on capitalist relations of production but also paid attention to precapitalist relations.

The comparison of views in Tables 2 and 3 highlights their similarities and contrasts. Most of the reformist and all of the revolutionary writers took a stand against imperialism; all certainly were concerned with the negative consequences of imperialism, and most favored some form of socialism, social democratic or revolutionary. Whereas the reformists expressed hope for the emerging national bourgeoisie, the revolutionaries carefully documented the failure of the national bourgeoisie in the face of imperialism. They all understood underdevelopment to be a consequence of dependency, and dependency for them was a reflection of capitalism's domination of periphery. All the writers adopted a structural approach by separating the advanced capitalist center from the backward and underdeveloped periphery. In their attention to capitalism, most focused on international markets and trade rather than on internal patterns of production. The reformist writers tended not to emphasize class struggle, although some of them used such categories of class as bourgeoisie and proletariat, national and international or imperialist bourgeoisies. In contrast, all the revolutionary writers referred to these and other class categories, although their attention to underdevelopment and dependency sometimes diverted them from an in-depth class analysis.

Another group of writers of this postwar period is distinguished from the reformists by an insistence on revolutionary socialism and from the revolutionaries by an emphasis on international markets and trade in the world system. Paul Baran addressed the implications of underdevelopment in the backward world. He believed that the dependent countries could not accumulate as the advanced countries had and could not overcome the obstacles of monopoly capitalism and imperialism. His theory of underdevelopment was related to underconsumption in the capitalist system, to a variety of economic surpluses, to backwardness, and to monopoly capital. The solution to these problems was socialism and revolution, and the Cuban Revolution served as an example.

The early thought of Baran was widely known in Latin America and other parts of the less advanced world. His formulation of a theory of underdevelopment influenced a number of later writers, in particular the distinction between two worlds, the idea of domination and backwardness, and the revolutionary thrust toward socialism as a way out. André Gunder Frank was especially attracted to this formulation. Frank divided the world into metropoles and satellites and showed that Latin American underdevelopment was the result of capitalism, not feudalism. Like Baran, he argued that capitalism operated differently in underdeveloped countries than in developed ones. Early in his work, Frank referred to the development of capitalism on a world scale and to the capitalist world system. He criticized those people who insisted that feudalism had caused underdevelopment in their countries along the path of autonomous national development. He discounted interpretations of a dual society, arguing that the backward and modern worlds were tied to a chain of world metropoles and satellites. He showed the impact of capitalism on the world system by referring to economic cycles and the devastation capitalism leaves in its wake.

Frank's early writing provided a foundation for much of the writing on underdevelopment, and his emphasis on capitalism and its consequences and on the world system seems to have influenced Immanuel Wallerstein to pursue some of these themes in his examination of European capitalism. Wallerstein concentrated on the transition from feudalism to capitalism in Europe and then traced the evolution of capitalism from the fifteenth century. His work identified a network of exchange relations on a world scale and the transfer of surplus from periphery to core. Samir Amin argued that the world was integrated into a commercial and financial network on a world scale, tied to a capitalist world market that also affected the socialist countries. Amin was concerned about accumulation, private accumulation, unevenness of productivity, disarticulation of economy, and dependence represented by outside domination. He adopted the structural dichotomy of center and periphery used by most of the writers on underdevelopment and concentrated on a theory of the periphery that he believed was not developed in the work of Marx, Lenin, and others. With his attention to capitalist social formations in the periphery, he intended to put aside misleading concepts of underdevelopment. He also attempted to focus on modes of production and questions of class. He argued for liberation of the periphery, autonomous accumulation, and a national, popular, democratic, and socialist direction. Arghiri Emmanuel, whose work influenced and also was criticized by Amin, attempted to build on analysis in the third volume of *Capital* by emphasizing relations of exchange rather than production.

Criticism and New Directions

The criticism of the views just summarized has, of course, been prolific and stimulating. Prebisch and his ECLA colleagues attacked some of the diffusionist theories of development but, in turn, found their own solutions for autonomous national development subject to debate. Frank exposed the weaknesses of mainstream development theory and also challenged some premises of the Communist parties, but his own assumptions were scrutinized by Marxist scholars (see Chilcote 1974 and Munck 1981 for reviews of these criticisms). Some critics attacked his emphasis on circulation and market and, in particular, his notion of transfer of surplus in capitalist Latin America since the fifteenth century (Assadourian et al. 1974, Booth 1975, Kay 1975, and Laclau 1971). Some questioned his exclusive schema and lack of concrete analysis (Henfrey 1981), and others considered his conception "ideological" (Leys 1977) or not Marxist (Leaver 1977). A proponent of Frank's theory might see his attention to underdevelopment as an alternative to Marxist orthodoxy (Foster-Carter 1976), although many writers recognized the weakness in his class analysis (Cueva 1976, 1977). Frank soon declared that the concept of dependency was "dead" and joined Wallerstein and others in analysis of the world system.

The positions of Frank on feudalism and capitalism, national bourgeoisie, and revolution of course provoked what might be considered more-orthodox Marxist criticisms of his theories. Bill Warren (1973) was one of the first to attack Frank on these grounds, and Raúl Fernández and José Ocampo (1974) initiated a debate with him over similar questions and warned that prevailing thought on dependency should be challenged. They were concerned about the neglect of feudalism and emphasized a traditional Leninist view of imperialism. Their essentially Stalinist position represented a defense of older ideas with a plea to return to the classical writings of Marx, Lenin, and Stalin rather than to become revisionist in thinking. Bernstein (1979) concluded that although radical underdevelopment theory had recognized the contradiction of capitalism and discredited models of modernization, it was essentially incompatible with historical materialism as differentiated from theoretical tendencies in bourgeois social science. John Weeks (1981) and Carlos Johnson (1981) identified the ideological assumptions of the theories of underdevelopment and dependency and argued that the new ideas were but imitations of old ones dating to the previous century.

Cardoso's stress on the study of concrete "situations" of dependency and his attempt to avoid rigid theoretical formulations leaned away from determinism in the direction of empirical generalizations and, for some people, away from Marxism altogether (Myer 1975). Ultimately, Cardoso abandoned most of his earlier ideas on dependent capitalist development (1977b, 1979b), but not before engaging in a debate with Marini (1978a) and being criticized by Weffort (1971).

Phillip O'Brien (1975) and, to a lesser extent, Colin Leys (1977) cautioned proponents of dependency theory not to exaggerate concepts that generalized everything but explained nothing, and this advice may have prompted some dependency thinkers to move in new directions. Despite his reservations, O'Brien acknowledged that dependency and underdevelopment were undoubtedly here to stay, a proposition also accepted by Sanjaya Lall (1975) and Ian Roxborough (1979) and evidenced by such spirited defenses as those of Dos Santos (1978) and Bambirra (1978).

Inherent in this and many of the criticisms of the past theories of underdevelopment and development are some important issues. First, there is the tendency of many writers to emphasize underconsumption as a cause of imperialism, that is, the idea that the industrialized nations need markets abroad to make up for the lack of demand for surplus production at home—or that the market in a less developed area is restricted by the consuming power of a dominant bourgeoisie whose numbers are small in comparison to the national population, thus accounting for backwardness (Lustig 1980). Second, it is evident that dependent relationships between dominant and backward countries can be conceptualized less as theory than as a condition between entities or a model that heuristically permits some comparison. Third, there is the issue of whether analysis of underdevelopment should emphasize relations of market and circulation or trade rather than relations of production. Fourth, some writings stress the need for an underdeveloped country to advance through capitalism and its contradictions before it can possibly achieve socialism, whereas other writers (for example, Thomas 1978) emphasize the noncapitalist path to socialism through revolution and confrontation with imperialism. These issues relate to the nature of imperialism, the material basis of society, and the possibility of class struggle. Central to the dialogue over these issues has been the question of the compatibility of dependency and underdevelopment approaches to a theory of Marxism (Chilcote 1981a).

Given the debate on the old and new theories, what of the future? Clearly, theories of underdevelopment will continue to be elaborated and debated. The work of Frank and Wallerstein on world system was an extension of some of the earlier work and a reassessment of capitalist development through history. Although effort in this direction undoubtedly will continue, other currents are having intellectual impact.

These include theories of internationalization of capital, modes and articulation of modes of production, and class struggle.

Internationalization of Capital

The theory of internationalization of capital has been elaborated by Christian Palloix (1975, 1977). Palloix attempts to extend the methodology and categories of *Capital* so as to permit an analysis of the movement of capital and class struggle on an international level. He focuses on such themes as the elements for the critique of political economy and the internationalization of capital, international valorization, modes of international accumulation of capital, and the internationalization of the productive and financial system. In this process, he reviews the relevant literature and criticisms of the theory.

Robert B. Cohen argues that Palloix has contributed in two important ways. First, he demonstrates "the logic of a radical analysis of the current stage of capitalism based upon the dynamics of the system itself, rather than focused exclusively, or nearly exclusively, upon the multinational corporation." Second, he shows "how volumes two and three of *Capital* can serve as the foundation for such an analysis, by more explicitly setting out capital and labor, the mode of accumulation and the social relations of production, as the key elements for any Marxian appraisal of the new world economy" (Cohen, introduction to Palloix 1977, 1). Palloix thus differs from most previous Marxists in that he looks at the exploitation of labor in the process of production on a world scale rather than at the extraction of surplus from the periphery. Cohen goes on to describe the uniqueness of Palloix's approach.

> Thus, in today's economy there is a new mode of accumulation of capital characterized by not only the internationalization of each of the circuits of capital, but also by: 1) an international differentiation of the working class through deskilling, differentiation of the labor process, and the differentiation of the production and reproduction of labor power and of the value of labor power; 2) the interlinking of national and international economies; 3) the operation of the law of value on an international level; and 4) the important role of nation-states in aligning internal, national conditions through the use of a monetary standard. [Palloix 1977, 2]

An interesting application of this theory is in Marcussen and Torp's reassessment of dependency and their recognition that new forms of internationalization of capital have appeared since the rise of oil prices in 1973 and the subsequent economic crisis in Europe. Their argument is that capital is being directed from Europe to the periphery in the search for new investments and markets. This activity has permitted a basis for national capital accumulation within capitalist development, a process that seems to be taking place in some countries while others continue to suffer from the blocked development characterized by the dependency school: "We have reached the conclusion that dynamic elements exist in the changing historical conditions for capital accumulation in the Western countries, particularly the economic crisis since 1973, and that these elements are responsible for the creation of new reproductive structures, in parts of the Periphery which may very well break with the 'blocked development' situation" (Marcussen and Torp, 1982, 10).

They examine changing patterns in the internationalization of capital, noting the increase of direct foreign investments by capitalist enterprises of the center in the developing countries; the rapid growth in the internationalization of other forms of capital, such as private and public export credits, bank loans, and commodity exports, with the intent of stimulating production and reproduction processes in the periphery; new forms of cofinancing the activities of multinational firms in the Third World; increasing imports of large producer plants and technology by the peripheral countries; and the changing character of the international division of labor, away from exports of raw materials and toward manufacturing activities.

Given these changing conditions, Marcussen and Torp argue that new forces have emerged in the periphery so that autonomous development might occur. Principal among these forces is the state, which assumes the role of the national bourgeoisie as a promoter of capitalism and, with the assistance of international financial institutions, establishes "the material preconditions for capitalist production (infrastructure, investment codes and legal framework, etc.)" and "extracts economic surpluses from, primarily, the agricultural sector" (Marcussen and Torp 1982, 12). Thus national accumulation of capital becomes possible within the periphery under the aegis of the state; the state becomes the "instrument" in the new capitalist production and reproduction that occur through the internationalization of capital. Marcussen and Torp illustrate this phenomenon by analyzing the impact of French capital in the Ivory Coast. They attempt to demonstrate that the Ivory Coast has the potential to transcend its condition of "blocked development," and they conclude with the view that "at least a few countries in the Periphery can develop into fully fledged capitalist social formations, resulting in a much more differentiated situation" (Marcussen and Torp 1982, 139).

There are, of course, other examples of works that argue along these lines. Some time ago, Stephen Hymer examined the multinational corporation in terms of international capital movements, including investments of corporations in overseas branches and subsidiaries as well as short- and long-term equity capital stimulated by the multinationals; international capitalist production, involving the incorporation of labor from many countries into an integrated world corporate structure of production; and international government, the result of the eroding power of national governments in the face of international economic policy and the tendency of the multinational corporation to internationalize labor and capital (Hymer 1972). Efforts to move in this direction are also evident in the work of Samir Amin, especially *Accumulation on a World Scale* (1974a), and Ernest Mandel in *Late Capitalism* (1975). David Barkin (1981) and Gary Howe (1981) also search for a theory of internationalization of capital.

Similar arguments are used by Bill Warren in *Imperialism: Pioneer of Capitalism* (1980), which emphasizes the progressive aspects of capitalism. Warren is concerned about "the reversal of Marx's own view of the progressive character of imperialism," and he wages a polemic in favor of the position that imperialism has been a progressive force capable of promoting industrialization and economic growth: "The unique achievements of capitalism, both cultural and material, must not be overlooked, particularly the fact that capitalism released individual creativity and organized cooperation in production." Capitalism also serves as the basis for an emerging socialism: "There is an importent connection between capitalism and parliamentary (bourgeois) democracy; the latter provides the best political environment for the socialist movement and creates conditions that favour a geniune learning process by the working class."

Lenin, Warren believes, distorted the Marxist assumption that capitalism could advance in precapitalist countries: "It was Lenin . . . who initiated the ideological process through which the view that capitalism could be an instrument of social advance in pre-capitalist societies was erased from Marxism. . . . Lenin was wrong about the alleged eonomically retrogressive effect in the industrialized countries of monopolization between 1870 and 1914." In short, Marxist analysis of imperialism was undermined by "the requirements of bourgeois anti-imperialist propaganda and, indirectly, what were thought to be the security requirements of the Soviet state." Lenin's theory of imperialism was transferred to "the underdevelopment fiction" to meet the "psychological needs and political requirements of Third World nationalists." "The more recent theories of 'underdevelopment' are best regarded as postwar versions of Lenin's *Imperialism*."

Warren goes on to argue that contrary to current Marxist views, the prospects for capitalist development in many underdeveloped countries are favorable, both in capitalist agriculture and industry. Even under colonialism, capitalist development was advanced; likewise, since the Second World War, there has been an upsurge in capitalist social relations and productive forces in the Third World: "Capitalism has struck deep roots there and developed its own increasingly vigorous internal dynamic." Obstacles to development are found, not between imperialism and the Third World, but in "the internal contradictions of the Third World itself." The relationship of developed countries with underdeveloped countries results in the industrialization and development of the latter. Thus ties of subordination or dependence are being loosened, not tightened: "The distribution of political-economic power within the capitalist world is thereby growing less uneven . . . although one dimension of imperialism is the domination and exploitation of the non-communist world by a handful of major advanced capitalist countries . . . we are nevertheless in an era of declining imperialism and advancing capitalism" (Warren 1980, 7–10).

Specifically, Warren raises a number of objections to the theories of dependency and underdevelopment. He argues that dependency theory is "static"; the paradigm of center and periphery, "largely unexamined"; and the influence of peripheral economies upon the core countries, not yet explored. He considers the *dependentista* approach incorrect in its characterization of imperialism as a monolithic structure and in its equation of imperialism with the world market, thus excluding "by definition the possibility of any non-dependent capitalist Third World progress" (Warren 1980, 163–165).

Modes and Articulation of Modes of Production

The roots of the modes of production approach may be found in Marx's focus on the material base of society as described in the *Preface to the Critique of Political Economy*; in the references to stages in the evolution of human society, mentioned in *The Communist Manifesto* and *The German Ideology*; and in his analysis of precapitalist modes of production in sections of the *Grundrisse*. Trotsky advocated the law of combined and uneven development, suggesting the need to examine modes of production in juxtaposition. Lenin's early writings on Russian capitalism recognized the clash of different modes and processes in the transition to capitalism, especially in the countryside, and he was interested in analyzing class struggles and possible class alliances.

Recent advocacy of a theory of modes of production has emanated from a variety of sources. There was the classic debate between Maurice Dobb and Paul Sweezy on feudalism and capitalism (Hilton et al. 1976); the debate between Sweezy and Bettelheim on the transition to socialism (1971); and the theoretical critiques by Hindess and Hirst (1975, 1977). However, it was the work of French structuralists, especially in economic anthropology, that caught the attention of social scientists (see Clammer 1975 for an introduction to French contributions; one of the most useful syntheses of the literature is Foster-Carter 1978).

The French Marxist writers employ the language and methodology of Louis Althusser and Etienne Balibar, particularly the notion of articulation in their attention to modes of production. Articulation means joining together, that is, combining different modes of production, but it also implies the dialectical relationship between the economic base and the political superstructure. Although Althusser and Balibar never use the term "articulation of modes of production," it has become common usage (Foster-Carter 1978, 53), probably because of the writing of another French thinker, Pierre-Philippe Rey, who explicitly incorporates the term into his theory (Rey 1973). Rey's work is not translated into English, but a brief summary of his ideas may help.

Rey uses articulation to explain that history does not necessarily evolve unilinearly from one stage to another of development but that old and new modes are evident in the transition, say from feudalism to capitalism. Brewer restates Rey's position: "Two modes of production cannot be seen as coexisting within a transitional social formation entirely independent of each other, just sitting side by side. . . . The two modes of production are in contradiction, in the sense that one will replace the other, but at the same time, during the period of transition, each must be reproduced, so that the conditions of their reproduction must be compatible with each other" (Brewer 1980, 184).

Rey uses this conception to show the differences in development between Europe and the Third World. He believes that capitalism will eventually destroy all relations of exploitation that characterize precapitalist modes of production, although socialist revolution may intervene before capitalism has completed its course. In this sense, he does not accept the view that dependent capitalism in the periphery operates as its own mode of production and laws of motion, as suggested by Amin (1976b); nor does he agree with the view of Geoffrey Kay (1975) that capital foments underdevelopment because it does not exploit the underdeveloped world enough.

For Rey, three stages of articulation are evident in the process of development (Foster-Carter 1978, 59–60). At the outset, the traditional, or precapitalist, mode remains dominant; capitalism may draw raw materials from it, but this exchange tends to reinforce the precapitalist mode, not promote capitalist relations of production. Then, as there is a shift in the relationship between the two modes, capitalism becomes dominant in the transition from feudalism; peasant agriculture and handicrafts are partially transformed and then completely eliminated as a labor force emerges. Finally, once capitalism is able to nurture its own labor supply, it has evolved into a third stage not yet known to the Third World. (See Bradby 1975 for a summary and elaboration of Rey's theory.)

Attention to modes of production was partially a response to the theories of underdevelopment and dependency emerging in Latin America. In particular, Laclau distinguished between dependency and mode of production in his attack on Frank (Laclau 1971). Laclau stressed relations of production rather than market relations and argued that in Latin America, precapitalist modes of production exist alongside the capitalist mode.

French structuralism has influenced several Latin American theorists to study agricultural society with a modes of production approach. Domenico Sindico refers to Althusser's notion of an economic and social formation as the result of at least two modes of production, one dominant and the other subordinate, in combination and determining the form of the legal and political and ideological superstructure of society (Sindico 1977, 98–99). Roger Bartra has argued that the mode of production must be analyzed on a concrete, not an abstract, level of society (Bartra 1975b). Both Sindico (1980) and Bartra (1975a) have applied their theory to investigation in the Mexican countryside, Montoya (1982) has studied class relations in rural Peru, and two Bolivians, Rojas (1980) and Rodriguez (1980), have examined the question of subsumption of labor (raised by Marx in a previously unpublished essay but now included as an appendix to the Vintage edition of the first volume of *Capital* [Marx 1977]). Richard Harris (1979) has provided an overview of the literature emanating from the structuralist school in Latin America, while Norma Chinchilla and James Dietz (1981) have showed how mode of production analysis transcends the early work on underdevelopment and dependency.

John Taylor's *From Modernization to Modes of Production* (1979) is an effort to offer a structuralist view of history using the modes of production approach. He offers a reinterpretation of the Latin American experience and argues that different modes of production can be intertwined in social formations in such a way that the feudal mode imposed by merchant capital obstructs contemporary capitalism and imperialism; thus merchant capital under the control of a feudal oligarchy prevented the spread of modern capitalism into agriculture in Latin

America. The notion of underdevelopment, he argues, is "teleological" and "economistic" and thus offers no "rigorous basis for analyzing the existence, forms, or effects of the various types of capitalist penetration within societies dominated by non-capitalist modes of production." Contemporary reality can be understood, he says, on the basis of "historical materialism as *a social formation which is dominated by an articulation of (at least) two modes of production*—a capitalist and a non-capitalist mode—in which the former is, or is becoming, increasingly dominant over the other." Within the Third World, it is necessary to study "the development of a social formation in which a non-capitalist mode is dominant"; further, the social formation in the Third World not only is determined by "an articulation of modes of production" but is "characterized by a whole series of *dislocations* between the various levels of the social formation." These dislocations and imperialism under specific conjunctures can create the preconditions for a socialist mode of production: "There can be no such thing as a 'linear succession' from dominance by a capitalist mode of production. Imperialist penetration, having as its object to create the preconditions for a transition to a specific form of capitalist production, can produce— as we shall see later—the preconditions for the possibility of a socialist mode of production" (Taylor 1979, 101–103).

Although expressing enthusiasm for the modes of production approach, Colin Henfrey characterizes Taylor's analysis as "a single, suspended history" in which "there are no mediating concepts like accumulation and class formation," and "class relations and indeed the whole of history appear to be given by the modes of production" (Henfrey 1981, 41). Henfrey believes that the structuralist conception of modes of production represents an advance over the historically determinist Stalinist perspective, which emphasizes modes as mere linear stages of development. In particular, writers such as Balibar (1970) see modes of production as theoretical constructs rather than as linear stages, but they also fail to apply their conception to particular realities.

Anthony Brewer, in his *Marxist Theories of Imperialism*, has attempted to offer a grand synthesis of the various theories of development and underdevelopment. He believes that Marxist theories of capitalist development can be divided between those that focus on the progressive impact of capitalism in developing the forces of production and those that emphasize the negative consequences of capitalism. This dichotomy is similar to my own approach in the present volume.

Brewer systematically reviews the major writers who have followed these two modes of thinking and argues that there is no particular level of analysis to be emphasized, that an adequate study of the world system must examine unit of production, nation-state, and the world system itself. He considers the debate over modes of production meaningless.

> The classical Marxists defined modes of production in terms of the relation between the direct producers and their immediate exploiters, and simultaneously treated them as successive stages of social development. This approach does not work well when applied to underdeveloped countries. One answer is to redefine modes of production as stages of development on a world level and to deny the relevance of production relations as they are usually defined, but this leaves little to put in their place. The alternative is to modify the conception of modes of production as successive stages by arguing that a variety of relations of production can coexist within a single society. In itself, this step only provides a framework for analysis. [Brewer 1980, 273]

In discussing the issue of relations of production in an assessment of development or underdevelopment, Brewer suggests that they are significant for some authors whereas others stress criteria such as extraction of surplus or unequal exchange. He concludes "that a single explanation is unlikely to apply to all cases at all stages of development, so that a complete theory may draw on both views" (Brewer 1980, 273). Brewer also warns of the tendency of Marxist writers to argue that U.S. dominance in the capitalist world will continue and that the underdeveloped countries have little hope of developing without breaking completely with the world capitalist system. He suggests that European and Japanese capital may challenge U.S. dominance and establish new industrial centers in low-wage areas. However, he is optimistic about Marxist theory: "Considerable progress has been made and there is a real prospect of creating an integrated Marxist analysis of world economy" (Brewer 1980, 294).

Toward a Theory of Class Struggle

My review of the theories of development and underdevelopment has surveyed the literature, ideas, and criticisms along several lines of thinking. Figure 1 depicts these tendencies. In the early stages, there was concern with the diffusionist and modernization theories. There also was attention to the inadequacies of theories of imperialism: They did not yield analysis of internal structure and conditions. Thus the

130

FIGURE 1

Old and New Directions of Developmental Theory

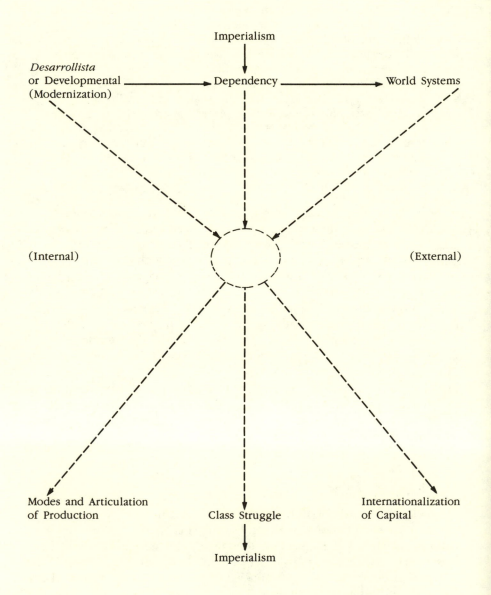

idea of dependency in its many forms was posited to account for both internal and external conditions affecting underdevelopment.

Also in the early stages, dichotomies appeared in the literature. Most important was the difference between progressive and regressive interpretations of capitalism; thus developmental perspectives argued that the promotion of capitalism in the Third World would bring progress, whereas views of dependency portrayed capitalism as creating underdevelopment. The latter position was carried on in the theory of world system, while the former evolved through the theory of inter-nationalization of capital. The inadequacies of the dependency and world system theories were addressed by those theorists who turned to analysis of modes and articulation of modes of production. All these orientations embraced structural frameworks by using such formulations as center and periphery.

A generation ago, it was common for critics to note the inadequacies of development theory and urge the employment of a class analysis and a search for a theory of class struggle. During the intervening years, a dearth of such analysis has been evident, and inadequacies and frustrations in the search for new theory have not been resolved by recent effort. Henfrey has advocated that theory be integrated with real social history. He suggests that neither the dependency nor the modes of production approach will meet this test. Instead, the task will be "relating a theory of imperialism to the histories of the exploited classes" (Henfrey 1981, 49). Dale Johnson argues that "reversion to a theory of imperialism ignores the great contribution of the dependency literature," but he urges "a class analysis under conditions of dependence" and the need to understand that "history always reverts to the never-ending struggle of ordinary people, oppressed by the objective circumstances presented to them" (Dale Johnson 1981, 110, 116; elaborated in Chilcote and Johnson 1983). James Petras shows the weaknesses in world system theory and concludes that "world capitalist system can best be analyzed by examining the hegemonic class relationship and imperialist state and the conflicting class relationships that emerge in each social formation" (Petras 1981, 153). He calls for focus on the social relations of production, redefinition of political economy away from development to exploitation, and a look at class relationships on both the internal and the international levels. His approach would locate the process of capital accumulation within the context of state and class relationships. Accumulation, he believes, is essentially a global problem, related to movement of capital and the activity of multinational corporations: "These movements and activities can best be understood through the notion of the imperial state, the worldwide political network which facilitates the growth and expansion of capital" (Petras 1981, 154).

I hope that my effort to bring together the disparate threads of theory will stimulate readers to seek answers to profound questions, and to this end I have attempted to sort out the various currents of thought. The more important task is the continuing elaboration of theory and examination of real situations for a deeper understanding of capitalism and socialism in the contemporary world.

Notes

1. An example of a work that entraps itself in geographical classification is Jalée (1968). For a critical review of this otherwise useful book, see Nuti (1969).

2. Wolf-Phillips (1979), 105, cites A. Angelopoulos for a reference to Alfred Sauvy.

3. Peter Worsley, "How Many Worlds?" in Wolf-Phillips et al. (1980), 15, and Joseph L. Love, "'Third World': A Response to Professor Worsley," in Wolf-Phillips et al. (1980), 30.

4. The committee published its early deliberation in Almond and Coleman (1960).

5. Support for Nkrumah's position is found in Chaliand (1978), which exposes the myths of the Third World concept and criticizes the belief that armed struggle can create the conditions for popular revolution.

6. The Maoist theory of three worlds is described in *Peking Review* 20 (November 4, 1977), 11, 17, and there is a critical discussion of it in Muni (1979).

7. The Albanian position was published as "The Theory and Practice of Revolution" in the July 7, 1977, issue of the Tirania newspaper *Zeri i popullit* and reprinted as "Albania Party Challenges," *Guardian* (New York) 29 (July 27, 1977), 16–17.

8. Grant McCall, "Four Worlds of Experience and Action," in Wolf-Phillips et al. (1980), 40–43.

9. My description of capitalism closely follows that of Mandel (1977). Mandel identifies the features of capitalism as commodity production, for sale on the market; private ownership of the means of production; competition to gain the largest share of the market; maximization of profit; and accumulation of capital. Following Marx, Mandel mentions laws of motion of capitalism: the concentration and centralization of capital; the progressive proletarianization of the working population; the growth in the organic composition of capital (constant capital to buy machines, buildings, and raw materials and variable capital to buy labor power); the tendency of the average rate of profit to fall; the objective socialization of production; the inherent contradictions of the capitalist mode of production; and the periodic crisis of overproduction (see Mandel [1977], 43–54).

10. Dahl (1971) and Rose (1967) are representative of this mainstream literature.

11. Marx never fully elaborated a theory of class. Only in the brief and incomplete last chapter of the third volume of *Capital* did he offer a conception: "Wage labourers, capitalists and landowners constitute the three big classes of modern society based upon the capitalist mode of production" ([1967],

3:885). However, Marx recognized the existence of other classes. In *The Class Struggles in France, 1848–1850* and *The Eighteenth Brumaire of Louis Bonaparte*, he identified the finance aristocracy, industrial bourgeoisie, petty bourgeoisie, peasantry, lumpen proletariat, industrial proletariat, bourgeois monarchy, and large bourgeoisie.

12. For elaboration of the differences between Marx and Weber, see Chilcote (1981b), 81–135.

13. An especially useful effort to review conceptions of class is Wright (1980); also see Dos Santos (1970a).

14. See the last in a series of studies on political development sponsored by the Social Science Research Council: Binder et al. (1971).

15. Probably the best-known work in nationalism and development is Deutsch (1953). Other works on the topic include Emerson (1960).

16. Mohri sides with Davis (1967a), 14, 16. See also Davis (1967b), especially Chapter 3.

17. The literature of underdevelopment in the Third World emphasizes the negative consequences of capitalism. Benachehou (1980) discussed the failure of various protectionist practices such as import substitution and the discouraging of foreign imports. He found that only 10 of 123 nations have manufacturing activity consisting of more than 20 percent of their gross domestic product and that production is not well diversified in the face of the activity of multinational firms and technological dependence. He argued for a new strategy in which industrialization would be geared to the internal markets with emphasis on transforming agrarian structures through pricing and income policies: control and coordination of the purchase of technologies from abroad, the promotion of technical education within the dependent nations, and control and coordination of financial resources from abroad. He argued for a popular and autonomous industrialization and for a more active role for the landless and poor peasantry and greater political initiative for the popular urban strata. His proposals resemble past and present reformist schemes that have done little to alter the conditions of nations in the Third World.

18. Letter, Marx to Engels, November 30, 1867, in Marx (1974), 161.

19. This position on merchant and industrial capital is reinforced by Kay (1975), who argues that merchant capital "was constitutionally incapable of consummating the process that it set in motion. It could never overcome its specific nature of merchant capital and realize its general nature as capital; it could never break out of the sphere of circulation and impose the law of value directly on the sphere of production. It corroded the feudal order but in the last analysis was always dependent upon it. It was revolutionary and conservative at the same time. It opened the way for industrial capitalism but also blocked its progress" (p. 97).

20. A very useful analysis of these events and Trotskyism in Latin America is in Hodges (1974)—see Chapter 3, "Latin American Trotskyism," pp. 67–135.

21. From mimeographed class notes of Prebisch's lectures at the University of Buenos Aires in 1944; cited by Love (1980), 68 n.37.

22. Known as the ECLA Manifesto, Prebisch's theses were set forth in *The Economic Development of Latin America and Its Principal Problems,*

published under a Spanish title in May 1949. Hirschman (1961) labeled this writing the ECLA Manifesto—mentioned in Love (1980), 57.

23. Although Love states that Manoilesco presented views similar to those of ECLA, he acknowledges that they had no direct influence on it. Theorists of corporatism drew upon Manoilesco's *Le siècle du corporatisme*, published in 1934.

24. Among his writings are Perroux (1962) and articles in *Economie Appliquée* (April-September 1958), *Quarterly Journal of Economics* (1949), and others cited in note 5 of his article on Latin America—see Perroux (1968), 97.

25. For a comprehensive review of Sunkel's ideas, see Sunkel with Paz (1970). For a useful discussion of how past and present development theories relate to Sunkel's conception, see Sunkel (1977).

26. The father collected and published Indian stories in his *Cuentos indígenas*, 2d ed. (Mexico: Instituto de Investigaciones Históricas, Universidad Nacional Autónoma de México, 1965). See in that volume the bibliographical discussion of Carlos Martínez Marín, "Bibliografía de Don Pablo González Casanova," pp. ix–xxv.

27. See González Casanova (1950).

28. González Casanova, interview with Joseph A. Kahl—see Kahl (1976), 76. On pp. 74–127, Kahl has provided an excellent synthesis of the life and thought of González Casanova as well as a list of his publications from 1948 to 1972.

29. See the summaries in Kahl (1976) and Chilcote and Edelstein (1974), 66–68. By 1980, given a deteriorating economy and the failure of the government party to effectively involve the masses in politics, González Casanova (1982) wrote about the prospects for a leftist coalition of parties and groups, arguing that its success was dependent on the support of workers in autonomous unions and of people on the local level; essential was an independent, revolutionary, and popular movement oriented toward mass action, articulation of mass interests, and increase of mass consciousness.

30. Kahl states, "Thus the proper direction of political action for progressive capitalists as seen from this perspective is the same as that for sensible radicals as deduced from Marxism-Leninism: struggle for the democratization of political and industrial institutions simultaneously with economic growth. Each is vital to the other, and the advice to the government and the bourgeoisie is clear; their long-run interests are on the side of more popular participation in national life, not on the side of authoritarian repression that would lead to economic stagnation" ([1976], 91).

31. González Casanova, "El colonialismo interno," (1970b), 221–250. Translated into English and published as "Internal Colonialism and National Development" in Horowitz, Castro, and Gerassi (1969), 118–139. González Casanova cites C. Wright Mills for an earlier use of internal colonialism. According to Mills, "the developed sections in the interior of the underdeveloped world—in the capital and in the coast—are a curious species of imperialistic power which has, in its own way, internal colonies" (Horowitz, Castro, and

Gerassi [1969], 120, from C. Wright Mills, *Power, Politics, and People*, ed. Irving Louis Horowitz [New York: Oxford University Press, 1963], p. 154). According to Stone (1979), the concept of internal colonialism was used during the 1930s to characterize relations between the North and South in the United States. For the use of internal colonialism in situations in the United States, see Blauner (1969), Donald J. Harris (1972), Almaguer (1971), and Moore (1970).

32. González Casanova, in Horowitz, Castro, and Gerassi (1969), 136. See the appendix, pp. 137–139, for a listing of forms and characteristics of internal colonialism.

33. González Casanova (1978). An earlier work examined U.S. ideology and foreign investment in Latin America—see González Casanova (1955).

34. González Casanova, ed. (1977). Vol. 2, dealing with Mexico, Central America, and the Caribbean was not available to me. González Casanova also edited a collection of essays on underdevelopment—see González Casanova (1970b).

35. Kahl (1976), 129–194, provides a biography and analysis of Cardoso's life and thought. Cardoso was born in 1931 in Rio de Janeiro, the son of a military man who had participated in the abortive revolt of the *tenentes*, or lieutenents, in 1922 and who later became minister of war. Kahl traces Cardoso's education, the influence of Roger Bastide and Florestán Fernandes, his early association with the Communist journal, *Fundamentos*, his early writings on slavery, and the evolution of his thinking about the concept of new dependency.

36. A chapter of this work was published in Cardoso (1968).

37. Cardoso acknowledged the influence of José Medina Echavarría, a Spanish sociologist who was director of the Latin American Institute for Social and Economic Planning in Santiago, Chile. While in Chile, Cardoso associated with Chilean economists Aníbal Pinto and Osvaldo Sunkel, who were also associated with the UN institute and had begun to write on dependency—see Kahl (1976), 138.

38. No effort is made here to review most of Cardoso's other writings, since the lines of his thinking are clearly presented in material available in English. Among sources the curious student may wish to delve into, however, is his earlier work on the entrepreneur in Brazil, which was expanded to focus on the entrepreneur in Argentina during 1965 and 1966. As adjunct director of the Latin American Institute in Santiago, Cardoso, in collaboration with Luciano Martins and Juan Carlos Marin, coordinated this research, then wrote up an analysis in Paris during 1967 and 1968—see Cardoso (1971b). Chapter 5 of that work reports on results of questions of dependency, development, and ideology. For the Spanish version, see Cardoso (1971a). Other books include Cardoso (1972b), a collection of essays presented at various institutions outside Brazil. Cardoso and Francisco Weffort edited a collection of essays on Latin America—see Cardoso and Weffort (1970). Also available is an essay, Cardoso (1977a).

39. Cardoso and Faletto (1979), ix, also refer to studies of Medina Echavarría and intellectuals in universities and political movements in São Paulo, Mexico, Buenos Aires, and Caracas.

40. The preface to the English edition is a synthesis and summary of developments beyond the original writing.

41. For a review of the work of Cardoso and Faletto, see Caporaso (1980).

42. Cardoso's essay was published in an earlier version—see Cardoso (1973c), 6–17. A less clear overview of some of these implications of dependency is in Cardoso (1972–1973). The Portuguese version of Cardoso's essay was included as "Imperialismo e dependência na América Latina," in Cardoso (1972b), 186–203.

43. This paper had been published in *Revista Latinoamericana de Ciencias Sociales* 4 (December 1972), 3–31, and was later reprinted in Cardoso (1980), 57–87.

44. Interview with Marcos Kaplan, Rio de Janeiro, August 14, 1982.

45. Rodolfo Ghioldi, in the March 16, 1947, edition of the Communist daily, *La Hora*, in Buenos Aires.

46. The Portuguese original of this book is Prado Júnior (1963).

47. In a later work, Prado Júnior argued that a different "duality" was evident in agriculture. Two types of rural activities prevailed in Brazil. One he called the *alta expressao comercial*, or commercial activity involving rubber and nuts in the Amazon, sugar in the Northeast, cacao in Bahia, coffee in São Paulo, and so on. The other was *actividades subsidiárias*, or subsistance production by local peoples (see Prado [1969]).

48. A summary of Vania Bambirra's work in Chile is Bambirra (1974). Her defense of a theory of dependency and rejoinder to a number of critics, including Agustín Cueva, Octavio Rodrígues, and Enrique Semo, is in Bambirra (1978).

49. Other writings in English by Dos Santos include Dos Santos (1974) and (1970a).

50. See also Dos Santos (1967).

51. Details of Dos Santos's conceptualization and criticism of bourgeois solutions are in Dos Santos (1970c).

52. Marini (1973b). Also see his essay in Marini et al. (1973).

53. Marini offered a critique of reformism, illustrating the case of the 1973 coup in Chile, in Marini (1976).

54. Quijano, in an interview with me in July 1964, revealed that his thinking tended to follow in the tradition of Marxist and Trotskyist thought.

55. Although Quijano continued to pay attention to dependency, in his later writings his analysis focuses on imperialism and the impact and response of the working classes in Peru and Latin America. Some of these writings include Quijano (1975, 1976b, 1976a, 1972).

56. Quijano (1977). Discussion of the Marxist emphasis on the reserve army of unemployed is in Quijano's introduction, pp. 7–30.

57. The United Secretariat of the Trotskyist Fourth International (for example, Fourth International [1978]) has consistently used terms as dependency and underdevelopment in referring to such countries as Brazil and South Korea that have undergone some industrialization or to the rivalry between imperialist and dependent capitalist countries. The terminology in all these instances

resembles that employed by writers of works on underdevelopment and dependency, but close examination also finds its origins in the thought of Leon Trotsky.

58. On the jacket of one of Vitale's books, the following works by him are identified: *Los discursos de Clotario Blest y la revolución; Historia del movimiento obrero;* and *Obras escogidas de Luis E. Recabarren.* In addition, he published Vitale (1963).

59. See for example, Mandel (1970b). Also for a discussion of basic concepts, see Mandel (1977).

60. See, for example, Mandel (1968). This work attempts to synthesize and clarify concepts and ideas in Marx's *Capital.* Volume 1 covers labor, necessary product, and surplus product; exchange, commodity, and value; money, capital, and surplus value; development and contradictions of capitalism; trade, credit, and money; agriculture; reproduction and growth of the national income; and periodical crises. Volume 2 focuses on monopoly capitalism and imperialism; capitalist decline; the Soviet economy; the economy of the transition period; socialist economy; and the origin, rise, and withering away of political economy. As to the last theme, Mandel argued that for Marx, political economy was essentially an ideology that will wither away together with the categories it attempts to explain. "What is certain is that, by virtue of the questions it will seek to answer, it will have little in common with past and present economic theory, with bourgeois political economy, or with the Marxist criticism of it. Marxist economists can claim the honour of being the first category of men of learning to work consciously towards the abolition of their own profession" (Mandel [1968], 2:730).

61. Among the polemical writings by Mandel are (1978a, 1978b, 1972, 1974, 1970a, 1978c, 1978d).

62. See Mandel (1975). Other works of historical synthesis include Mandel, ed. (1968) and Mandel (1979). Mandel also wrote the introductions to the Vintage edition and translation of Marx's *Capital,* 3 volumes published in 1977–1981.

63. Mandel cites figures provided by Samir Amin that the loss suffered by colonial and semicolonial countries during the middle sixties was approximately $22 billion annually (Mandel [1975], 346).

64. Biographical details on the life and thought of Paul Baran are in Sweezy and Huberman (1965), which was published as the March 1965 issue of *Monthly Review;* see especially Paul M. Sweezy's "Paul Alexander Baran: A Personal Memoir," pp. 28–62.

65. Also see Baran's "On the Nature of Marxism," pp. 19–42 in Baran (1969); this essay was originally published as two articles in the October and November 1958 issues of *Monthly Review.*

66. For Baran's view on underconsumption theory, see "Reflections on Underconsumption," pp. 185–202 in Baran (1969); this essay orignally was included in Moses Abramovitz et al., *The Allocation of Economic Resources* (Stanford: Stanford University Press, 1959).

67. Baran, "The Concept of the Economic Surplus," Chapter 2, pp. 22–43, in Baran (1960); quotes on pp. 23, 41.

68. Baran, "On the Roots of Backwardness," Chapter 5, pp. 134–162, in Baran (1960); quote on p. 134.

69. In an appendix, "Estimating the Economic Surplus," pp. 369–391, Joseph D. Phillips provided estimates of the U.S. surplus and its composition.

70. Paul A. Baran, "Reflections on the Cuban Revolution," in Baran (1969), 390. Originally most of this essay was published in the January 1961 issue of *Monthly Review* and some additional comments were given over radio station KPFA in Berkeley on April 21 and May 4, 1961.

71. Frank (1969). Chapter 2, "Sociology of Development and Underdevelopment of Sociology," pp. 21–94, was originally published in the Summer 1967 issue of *Catalyst* and was also published as Frank (1971).

72. Frank (1969), Chapter 2, "Mr. Heilbroner's Rhetoric and Reality," pp. 125–136, a reply to Robert Heilbroner's "Counterrevolutionary America" published in the April 1967 issue of *Commentary*.

73. Ibid., Chapter 7, "Liberal Anthropology vs. Liberation Anthropology," pp. 137–145, originally published in the May 1968 issue of *Current Anthropology*.

74. A critique of González Casanova (1970a). The quote is from "The Mexican Democracy of Pablo González Casanova," Chapter 20, p. 332, in Frank (1969). This essay was originally published in the Autumn 1965 issue of *Historia y Sociedad.*

75. Frank (1969), 339, from a critique of Furtado's April 1963 essay in *Foreign Affairs.*

76. Frank (1969), Chapter 25, "Capitalist Underdevelopment or Socialist Revolution," pp. 371–409.

77. Students should find useful Frank's critical assessment of the differences between Weber and Marx and the relation of their thought to development and underdevelopment—see in particular, Frank (1975a).

78. Frank (1978b), 18–19. Here Frank mentions a two-volume unpublished work in collaboration with Said A. Shah.

79. One would assume that Wallerstein had once been stimulated by Frank's early writings, but in a letter to me, dated August 7, 1979, Wallerstein stated that he had never been a *dependentista* but was a world systems theorist—letter from Immanuel Wallerstein to Ronald H. Chilcote. Frank joined with Wallerstein, Amin, and Arrighi in another work, Amin et al. (1982).

80. Frank (1979). Frank also published an essay in the first issue of *Review*, a journal on world systems theory edited by Wallerstein—see Frank (1977b).

81. Frank (1981a, 1981b, 1981c).

82. David Booth quotes Frank as having trained under "the most reactionary wing of the American bourgeoisie"—see Booth (1975), 61. However, Frank did attack University of Chicago economists who assisted the Chilean dictatorship after the 1973 coup—see Frank (1976, 1974a).

83. This work was also published with a postscript by A. A. Babu by Howard University Press, 1974. After the assassination of Rodney in Guyana in 1980, Hashim Gibrill (1980) wrote a review of his work. In addition to his classic study on Europe in Africa, Rodney was known for several other works

on Africa (1967, 1970, 1975) and on Guyana (1981a). A useful discussion of Rodney as a person and thinker is in Campbell (1981). For one of Rodney's last pieces, see (1981b). Rodney's work also inspired a work on the capitalist development of black America—see Marable (1983).

84. In addition, he edited a work with Peter C.W. Gutkind—Wallerstein and Gutkind (1976). He also published Wallerstein (1966).

85. See also Braudel (1980, 1977, 1972–1973, 1973).

86. "The Impact of the Annales School on the Social Sciences," *Review* 1 (Winter-Spring 1978). Includes articles by Wallerstein, Charles Tilly, Norman Birnbaum, Fernand Braudel, and others. The editorial board of *Review* included Giovanni Arrighi, Melvyn Dubofsky, Neville Dyson-Hudson, Deborah Hertz, and Terence K. Hopkins; the quarterly journal was edited by Wallerstein.

87. These issues appeared respectively in Spring 1979, Fall 1979, and Winter 1981. Some examples of articles appearing in the journal with a focus on world system are Hopkins (1977) and Hopkins and Wallerstein (1977). The latter is an elaborate research proposal that identifies the following topics: core periphery, semiperiphery, unequal exchange, capital accumulation on the international level; imperialism, hegemony, and bourgeoisie-proletariat on the level of state system; cyclical systems; and secular trends.

88. See *Newsletter* no. 3 (July 1979), 1–2, published by the Fernand Braudel Center.

89. Vol. 1, *Social Change in the Capitalist World Economy* (1978), was edited by Barbara Hockey Kaplan; vol. 2, *The World System of Capitalism: Past and Present* (1979), was edited by Walter L. Goldfrank; vol. 3 *Processes of the World-System* (1980), was edited by Terence K. Hopkins and Immanuel Wallerstein; vol. 4, *Dynamics of World Development* (1981), was edited by Richard Rubinson. All volumes were published by Sage Publications in Beverly Hills, California.

90. The early essays were brought together in Wallerstein (1979).

91. See also Amin (1971 and 1975a). Some collaborative projects with others have included Amin et al. (1975) and Amin (1975b, 1979). He also wrote Amin (1974b).

92. Among other works by Bettelheim is Bettelheim (1974). Also, with others, he wrote Bettelheim (1975).

93. A further exposition of Emmanuel's thesis is in his rejoinder to criticism by Samuelson (1976), which appeared in Emmanuel (1977).

References

Almaguer, Tomás
    1971   "Toward the Study of Chicano Colonialism." *Aztlan* 2 (Spring), 7–21.

Almond, Gabriel, and James S. Coleman, eds.
    1960   *The Politics of Developing Areas.* Princeton: Princeton University Press.

Amin, Samir
    1970   *The Maghreb in the Modern World: Algeria, Tunisia, Morocco.* Harmondsworth, Eng.: Penguin.
    1971   *L'Afrique de l'Ouest bloquée, l'économie politique de la colonisation, 1880–1970.* Paris: Editions de Minuit.
    1973   *Neo-Colonialism in West Africa.* Harmondsworth, Eng.: Penguin; New York: Monthly Review Press.
    1974a   *Accumulation on a World Scale: A Critique of the Theory of Underdevelopment.* 2 vols. New York: Monthly Review Press.
    1974b   *La question paysanne et le capitalisme.* Paris: Editions Anthropos-Idep.
    1975a   *L'Agriculture africaine et capitalisme.* Paris: Editions Anthropos-Idep.
    1975b   *La crise de l'impérialisme.* Paris: Editions de Minuit.
    1976a   *Impérialisme et sous-développement en Afrique.* Paris: Editions Anthropos-Idep.
    1976b   *Unequal Development: An Essay on the Social Formations of Peripheral Capitalism.* New York: Monthly Review Press.
    1976–   "Social Characteristics of Peripheral Formations: An Outline for
    1977   an Historical Sociology." *Berkeley Journal of Sociology* 21:27–50.
    1977   *Imperialism and Unequal Development.* New York: Monthly Review Press; Hassocks: Harvester Press.
    1978a   *The Arab Nation.* London: Zed Press.
    1978b   *The Law of Value and Historical Materialism.* New York: Monthly Review Press.
    1979   *Le Tiers Monde et la gauche.* Paris: Seuil.
    1980   *Class and Nation, Historically and in the Current Crisis.* New York: Monthly Review Press.

Amin, Samir, et al.
    1975   *La planification du sous-développement: critique de l'analyse de projets.* Paris: Editions Anthropos-Idep.

Amin, Samir; Giovanni Arrighi; André Gunder Frank; and Immanuel Wallerstein
1982   *Dynamics of Global Crisis.* New York: Monthly Review Press.

Andrade, Manuel Correia de
1967   *Espaço, polarização e desenvolvimento: a teoria dos polos de desenvolvimento e a realidade nordestina.* Recife: Centro Regional de Administração Municipal.

Assadourian, Carlos Sempat, et al.
1974   *Modos de producción en América Latina.* No. 40. Córdoba, Argentina: Cuadernos de Pasado y Presente.

Baer, Werner
1969   "The Economics of Prebisch and ECLA." Pp. 203–218 in Charles Nisbet, ed., *Latin America: Problems in Economic Development.* New York: Free Press.

Bagú, Sergio
1949   *Economía de la sociedad colonial: ensayo de historia comparada de América Latina.* Buenos Aires: Librería "El Ateneo."
1952   *Estructura social de la colonia: ensayo de historia comparada de América Latina.* Buenos Aires: Libraría "El Ateneo."
1960   *Argentina en el mundo.* Buenos Aires: Fondo de Cultura Económica.
1969   *Evolución histórica de la estratificación social en la Argentina.* Caracas: Instituto de Investigaciones Económicas y Sociales.

Bagú, Sergio, et al.
1967   *El desarrollo cultural en la liberación de América Latina.* No. 1. Montevideo: Centro Estudiantes de Derecho, Biblioteca de Cultura Universitaria.
1975   "Las clases sociales del subdesarrollo." Pp. 9–52 in Sergio Bagú et al., *Problemas del subdesarrollo latinoamericano.* Mexico City: Editorial Nuestro Tiempo.

Balibar, Etienne
1970   "The Basic Concepts of Historical Materialism." Pp. 199–308 in Louis Althusser and Etienne Balibar, *Reading Capital.* London: New Left Books.

Bambirra, Vania
1974   *El capitalismo dependiente latinoamericano.* Mexico City: Siglo Veintiuno Editores.
1978   *Teoría de la dependencia: una anticrítica.* Mexico City: Ediciones Era.

Baran, Paul A.
1960   *The Political Economy of Growth.* New York: Prometheus.
1969   *The Longer View: Essays Toward a Critique of Political Economy.* New York: Monthly Review Press.

Baran, Paul A., and Paul M. Sweezy
1966   *Monopoly Capital: An Essay on the American Economic and Social Order.* New York: Monthly Review Press.

Barkin, David
1981   "Internationalization of Capital: An Alternative Approach." *Latin American Perspectives* 8 (Summer and Fall), 156–161.

Bartra, Roger
1975a   "Peasants and Political Power in Mexico: A Theoretical Approach." *Latin American Perspectives* 2 (Summer), 125–145.
1975b   "Sobre la articulación de modas de produción articulados o lucha de classe?" *Historia y Sociadad* 5 (Spring), 5–19.

Benachehou, Abellatif
1980   "For Autonomous Development in the Third World." *Monthly Review* 33 (July-August), 43–52.

Bernstein, Harry
1979   "Sociology of Underdevelopment vs. Sociology of Development?" Pp. 77–106 in David Lehman, ed., *Development Theory: Four Critical Essays.* London: Frank Cass.

Bettelheim, Charles
1974   *Le profit et les crises: une approche nouvelle des contradictions du capitalisme.* Paris: F. Maspero.
1975   *Un debat sur l'échange inégal: salaries, sous-développement, impérialisme.* Paris: F. Maspero.

Binder, Leonard, et al.
1971   *Crises and Sequences in Political Development.* Princeton: Princeton University Press.

Blauner, Robert
1969   "International Colonialism and Ghetto Revolt." *Social Problems* 16 (Spring), 393–408.

Block, Fred
1977   "Late Capitalism." *Insurgent Sociologist* 7 (Fall), 72–74.

Booth, David
1975   "André Gunder Frank: An Introduction and Appreciation." Pp. 50–85 in Ivar Oxaal, Tony Barnett, and David Booth, eds., *Beyond the Sociology of Development.* London: Routledge and Kegan Paul.

Bradby, Barbara
1975   "The Destruction of Natural Economy." *Economy and Society* 4 (May), 127–161.

Braudel, Fernand
1972–   *The Mediterranean and the Mediterranean World in the Age of*
1973   *Phillip II.* 2 vols. New York: Harper and Row.
1973   *Capitalism and Material Life, 1400–1800.* London: Weidenfeld and Nicolson.
1977   *Afterthoughts on Material Civilization and Capitalism.* Washington, D.C.: Johns Hopkins University Press.
1979   *Civilisation matérielle, économie et capitalisme: XVe–XVIIIe siècle.* Paris: Armand Colin.
1980   *On History.* Chicago: University of Chicago Press.

Brenner, Robert
1977   "The Origins of Capitalist Development: A Critique of Neo-Smithian Marxism." *New Left Review* 104 (July-August), 25–92.

Brewer, Anthony
1980   *Marxist Theories of Imperialism.* London: Routledge and Kegan Paul. Includes, among others, chapters on Amin, pp. 233–257, Baran, pp. 131–157, and Frank, Wallerstein, and the Dependency "Theorists," pp. 158–181.

Bronfenbrenner, Martin
1978   "A World Class Economist from Underdeveloped Africa." *Economic Development and Cultural Change* 27 (October), 195–201.

Campbell, Trevor
1981   "The Making of an Organic Intellectual: Walter Rodney (1942–1980)." *Latin American Perspectives* 8 (Winter), 49–63.

Caporaso, James A.
1980   "Dependency Theory: Continuities and Discontinuities in Development Studies." *International Organization* 39 (Autumn), 605–628.

Cardoso, Fernando Henrique
1962   *Capitalismo e escravidão no Brasil meridional: O negro na sociedade do Rio Grande do Sul.* São Paulo: Difusão Européia do Livro.
1964   *Empresário industrial e desenvolvimento econômico no Brasil.* São Paulo: Difusão Européia do Livro.
1967   "The Industrial Elite." Pp. 94–114 in Seymour Martin Lipset and Aldo Solari, eds., *Elites in Latin America.* New York: Oxford University Press. In Spanish, pp. 106–124 in Lipset and Solari, eds., *Elites y desarrollo en América Latina.* Buenos Aires: Paidos.
1968   *Cuestiones de sociología del desarrollo en América Latina.* Santiago, Chile: Editorial Universitaria.
1971a   *Ideologías de la burguesía industrial en sociedades dependientes (Argentina y Brasil).* Mexico: Siglo Veintiuno Editores.

1971b   *Política e desenvolvimento em sociedades dependentes: ideologias do empresariado industrial argentino e brasileiro.* Rio de Janeiro: Zahar Editores.

1972a   "Dependency and Development in Latin America." *New Left Review* 74 (July-August), 83–95.

1972b   *O modelo político brasileiro e outros ensaios.* São Paulo: Difusão Européia do Livro.

1972–
1973   "Industrialization, Dependency, and Power in Latin America." *Berkeley School of Sociology* 17:79–95.

1973a   "Associated-Dependent Development: Theoretical and Practical Implications." Pp. 142–176 in Alfred Stepan, ed., *Authoritarian Brazil: Origins, Policies, and Future.* New Haven: Yale University Press.

1973b   "Dependency Revisited." Lecture at University of Texas, Austin, April 19.

1973c   "Imperialism and Dependency in Latin America." Pp. 7–33 in Frank Bonilla and Robert Girling, eds., *Structures of Dependence.* Stanford, California: n.p.

1976   "Current Theses in Latin American Development and Dependency: A Critique." Occasional Papers no. 20. New York: New York University.

1977a   "Las clases sociales y la crisis política de América Latina." Pp. 206–237 in Raúl Benitez Zenteno, ed., *Clases sociales y crisis política en América Latina (Seminario de Oaxaca).* Mexico City: Siglo Veintiuno.

1977b   "The Consumption of Dependency Theory in the United States." *Latin American Research Review* 10:3, 7–24.

1979a   "Development Under Fire." Paper given at Instituto Latinoamericano de Estudios Transnacionales, Mexico City, in May.

1979b   "On the Characterization of Authoritarian Regimes in Latin America." Pp. 34–57 in David Collier, ed., *The New Authoritarianism in Latin America.* Princeton: Princeton University Press.

1980   *As idéias e seu lugar: ensaios sôbre as teorias do desenvolvimento.* No. 33. Petrópolis, Brazil: Cadernos CEBRAP, Editôra Vozes.

Cardoso, Fernando Henrique, and Enzo Faletto
    1969   *Dependencia y desarrollo en América Latina: ensayo de interpretación sociológica.* Mexico City: Siglo Veintiuno Editores.
    1979   *Dependency and Development.* Translated by Marjory Mattingly Urquidi. Berkeley: University of California Press.

Cardoso, Fernando Henrique, and Francisco Weffort
    1970   *América Latina: ensayos de interpretación soiológico-política.* Santiago, Chile: Editorial Universitaria.

Cardoso, Fernando Henrique, et al.
    1971   *Sôbre teoria e método em sociologia.* São Paulo: Edições CEBRAP.

Chaliand, Gérard
    1978   *Revolution in the Third World.* New York: Penguin.

Chase-Dunn, Chris
    1978a   "Unequal Development." *Insurgent Sociologist* 8 (Winter), 78–81.
    1978b   "Who Gets What and Why." *Working Papers for a New Society*
              (March-April), 80–86.

Chase-Dunn, Christopher, and Richard Rubinson
    1977   "Toward a Structural Perspective on the World-System." *Politics
              and Society* 7:4, 453–476.

Chilcote, Ronald H.
    1974   "Dependency: A Critical Synthesis of the Literature." *Latin Amer-
              ican Perspectives* 1 (Spring), 4–29.
    1981a   "Issues of Theory in Dependency and Marxism." *Latin American
              Perspectives* 8 (Summer and Fall), 3–16.
    1981b   *Theories of Comparative Politics: The Search for a Paradigm.*
              Boulder, Colo.: Westview Press.

Chilcote, Ronald H., and Joel C. Edelstein, eds.
    1974   *Latin America: The Struggle with Dependency and Beyond.*
              Cambridge, Mass.: Schenkman Publishing Company.

Chilcote, Ronald H.; Steve Gorman; Cis LeRoy; and Sara Sheehan
    1975   "Internal and External Issues of Dependency: Approach, Peda-
              gogical Method, and Critique of Two Courses on Latin America."
              Review of Radical Political Economics 6 (Winter), 80–94.

Chilcote, Ronald H., and Dale L. Johnson, eds.
    1983   *Theories of Development: Mode of Production or Dependency?*
              Beverly Hills, Calif.: Sage Publications.

Chinchilla, Norma Stoltz, and James Lowell Dietz
    1981   "Towards a New Understanding of Development and Underde-
              velopment." *Latin American Perspectives* 8 (Summer and Fall),
              138–147.

Clammer, John
    1975   "Economic Anthropology and the Sociology of Development." Pp.
              208–228 in Ivar Oxaal, Tony Barnett, and David Booth, eds.,
              Beyond the Sociology of Development. London: Routledge and
              Kegan Paul.

Clarkson, Stephen
    1972   "Marxism-Leninism as a System for Comparative Analysis of Un-
              derdevelopment." *Political Science Review* 11 (April), 124–137.

Cueva, Agustín
1976   "A Summary of 'Problems and Perspectives of Dependency Theory.'" *Latin American Perspectives* 3 (Fall), 12–16.
1977   *El desarrollo del capitalismo en América Latina.* Mexico City: Siglo Veintiuno Editores.

Cypher, James
1977   "The Third Historical Epoch of the Capitalist Mode of Production." *Insurgent Sociologist* 7 (Fall), 74–82.
1979   "The Internationalization of Capital and the Transformation of Social Formations: A Critique of the Monthly Review School." *Review of Radical Political Economics* 11 (Winter), 33–49.

Dahl, Robert A.
1971   *Polyarchy, Participation, and Opposition.* New Haven: Yale University Press.

Davis, Horace B.
1967a   "Capital and Imperialism: A Landmark in Marxist Theory." *Monthly Review* 18 (September), 14–21.
1967b   *Nationalism and Socialism: Marxist and Labor Theories of Nationalism to 1917.* New York: Monthly Review Press.

Deutsch, Karl W.
1953   *Nationalism and Social Communication: An Inquiry into the Foundation of Nationality.* New York: Technology Press of Massachusetts Institute of Technology and John Wiley and Sons.

Dos Santos, Theotonio
1967   *El nuevo carácter de la dependencia.* No. 6. Santiago, Chile: Cuadernos de Estudios Socioeconómicos, CESO.
1970a   "The Concept of Social Classes." *Science and Society* 34 (Summer), 166–193.
1970b   "Dependencia económica y alternativas de cambio en América Latina." *Revista Mexicana de Sociología* 32 (March-April), 417–463.
1970c   *Dependencia y cambio social.* No. 11. Santiago, Chile: Cuadernos de Estudios Socioeconómicos, CESO.
1970d   "The Structure of Dependence." *American Economic Review* 60 (May), 231–236.
1974   "Brazil: Origins of a Crisis." Pp. 415–490 in Ronald H. Chilcote and Joel C. Edelstein, eds., *Latin America: The Struggle with Dependency and Beyond.* Cambridge, Mass.: Schenkman Publishing Company.
1978   *Imperialismo y dependencia.* Mexico City: Ediciones Era.

Emerson, Rupert
1960   *From Empire to Nation.* Cambridge: Harvard University Press.

Emmanuel, Arghiri
1972   *Unequal Exchange: A Study of the Imperialism of Trade.* With additional comments by Charles Bettelheim. New York: Monthly Review Press.
1977   "Gains and Losses from the International Division of Labor." *Review* 1 (Fall), 87–108.

Fernández, Raúl A., and José F. Ocampo
1974   "The Latin American Revolution: A Theory of Imperialism, Not Dependence." *Latin American Perspectives* 1 (Spring), 30–61.

Foster-Carter, Aiden
1976   "From Rostow to Gunder Frank: Conflicting Paradigms in the Analysis of Underdevelopment." *World Development* 4 (March), 167–180.
1978   "The Modes of Production Controversy." *New Left Review* 107 (January-February), 47–77.

Fourth International, United Secretariat
1978   "The International Capitalist Economy at the End of 1977." *Intercontinental Press* 16 (January 9), 4–5.

Frank, André Gunder
1966   "The Development of Underdevelopment." *Monthly Review* 18 (September), 17–31.
1967   *Capitalism and Underdevelopment in Latin America: Historical Studies of Chile and Brazil.* New York: Monthly Review Press.
1969   *Latin America—Underdevelopment or Revolution: Essays on the Development of Underdevelopment and the Immediate Enemy.* New York: Monthly Review Press.
1971   *Sociology of Development and Underdevelopment of Sociology.* London: Pluto.
1972   *Lumpenbourgeoisie: Lumpendevelopment, Dependence, Class, and Politics in Latin America.* New York: Monthly Review Press.
1974a   *Carta abierta en el aniversario del golpe chileno.* Madrid: A. Corazón.
1974b   "Dependence Is Dead, Long Live Dependence and the Class Struggle: A Reply to Critics." *Latin American Perspectives* 1 (Spring), 87–106.
1975a   "Development and Underdevelopment in the New World: Smith and Marx vs. the Weberians." *Theory and Society* 2 (Spring), 431–466.
1975b   *On Capitalist Underdevelopment.* Bombay: Oxford University Press.
1976   *Capitalismo y genocidio económico: carta abierta a la Escuela de Economía de Chicago a propósito de su intervención en Chile.* Bilbao, Spain: Zero.

1977a   "Dependence Is Dead, Long Live Dependence and the Class Struggle: An Answer to Critics." *World Development* 5 (April), 355–370.

1977b   "Long Live Transideological Enterprise: The Socialist Economies in the Capitalist International Division of Labor." *Review* 1 (Summer), 91–140.

1978a   *Dependent Accumulation and Underdevelopment.* London: Macmillan. New York: Monthly Review Press, 1979.

1978b   *World Accumulation, 1492–1789.* New York: Monthly Review Press.

1979   *Mexican Agriculture, 1521–1630: Transformation of the Mode of Production.* Cambridge: Cambridge University Press.

1981a   *Crisis in the Third World.* New York: Holmes and Meier.

1981b   *Crisis: In the World Economy.* London: Heinemann.

1981c   *Reflections on the World Crisis.* New York: Monthly Review Press.

Frondizi, Silvio

1947   *La integración mundial, última etapa del capitalismo (respuesta a una crítica).* Buenos Aires: Praxis. 2d ed., 1954.

1957   *La realidad argentina: ensayo de interpretación sociológica.* 2d ed. 2 vols. Buenos Aires: Praxis.

1960   *La revolución cubana.* Montevideo: Editora Ciencias Políticas.

Furtado, Celso

1959   *Formação económica do Brasil.* Rio de Janeiro: Editôra Fundo de Cultura.

1963   *The Economic Growth of Brazil: A Survey from Colonial to Modern Times.* Translated by Ricardo W. de Aguiar and Eric Charles Drysdale. Berkeley and Los Angeles: University of California Press.

1964   *Development and Underdevelopment.* Translated by Ricardo W. de Aguiar and Eric Charles Drysdale. Berkeley and Los Angeles: University of California Press.

1965   *Diagnosis of the Brazilian Crisis.* Translated by Suzette Macedo. Berkeley and Los Angeles: University of California Press.

1970   *Economic Development of Latin America: Historical Background and Contemporary Problems.* Translated by Suzette Macedo. Cambridge: Cambridge University Press.

1971   "Dependencia externa y teoría económica." *El Trimestre Económico* 38 (April-June), 335–349.

1973   "The Concept of External Dependence in the Study of Underdevelopment." Pp. 118–123 in Charles K. Wilber, ed., *The Political Economy of Development and Underdevelopment.* New York: Random House.

1978   *A economia latino-americana.* 2d ed. São Paulo: Companhia Editôra Nacional.

1981   *O Brasil pós-milagre.* No. 45. Rio de Janeiro: Coleção Estudos Brasileiros, Paz e Terra.

George, C. H.
1980   "The Origins of Capitalism: A Marxist Epitome and a Critique of Immanuel Wallerstein's Modern World System." *Marxist Perspectives* 3 (Summer), 70–99.

Gerstein, Ira
1977   "Theories of the World Economy and Imperialism." *Insurgent Sociologist* 7 (Spring), 9–22.

Gibrill, Hashim
1980   "Europe and Africa." *Monthly Review* 32 (October), 51–56.

Glausser R., Kalki, and Luis Vitale
1974   *Acerca del modo de producción colonial en América Latina.* N.p.: Ediciones Tiempo Crítico.

González Casanova, Pablo
1950   "Ideología francesa sobre América Hispánica." Ph.D. dissertation, University of Paris.
1955   *La ideología norteamericana sobre inversiones extranjeras.* Mexico City: Instituto de Investigaciones Económicas, Universidad Nacional Autónoma de México.
1967   *Las categorías del desarrollo económico y la investigación en ciencias sociales.* Mexico City: Instituto de Investigaciones Sociales, Universidad Nacional Autónoma de México.
1970a   *Democracy in Mexico.* Translated by Danielle Salti. New York: Oxford University Press. Originally published as *La democracia en México.* Mexico City: Ediciones ERA, 1965.
1970b   *Sociología de la explotación.* 2d ed. Mexico City: Siglo Veintiuno Editores.
1978   *Imperialismo y liberación en América Latina: una introducción a la historia contemporánea.* Mexico City: Siglo Veintiuno Editores.
1979   *La reforma política y sus perspectivas.* Mexico City: Ediciones de la Gaceta Informativa de la Comisión Federal Electoral.
1982   *La nueva metafísica y el socialismo.* Mexico City: Siglo Veintiuno Editores.

González Casanova, Pablo, ed.
1970   *Sociología del desarrollo latinoamericano: una guia para su estudio.* Mexico City: Instituto de Investigaciones Sociales, Universidad Nacional Autónoma de México.
1977   *América Latina: historia de medio siglo.* Mexico City: Siglo Veintiuno Editores. Vol. 1, *América del Sur.*

González Casanova, Pablo, and Guillermo Bonfil
1968   *Las ciencias sociales y la antropología: dos ensayos.* Mexico City: Centro Nacional de Productividad.

Hamalian, L., and F. R. Karl, eds.
1976   *The Fourth World: The Imprisoned, the Poor, the Sick, the Elderly, and the Underaged in America.* New York: Dell Publishing.

Harris, Donald J.
1972   "The Black Ghetto as Colony: A Theoretical Critique and Alternative Formulation." *Review of Black Political Economy* 2 (Summer), 1–33.

Harris, Richard L.
1979   "The Influence of Marxist Structuralism on the Intellectual Left in Latin America." *Insurgent Sociologist* 9 (Summer), 62–73.

Henfrey, Colin
1981   "Dependency, Modes of Production, and the Class Analysis of Latin America." *Latin American Perspectives* 8 (Summer and Fall), 17–54.

Hilton, Rodney, et al.
1976   *The Transition from Feudalism to Capitalism.* London: New Left Books.

Hindess, Barry, and Paul Q. Hirst
1975   *Pre-Capitalist Modes of Production.* London: Routledge and Kegan Paul.
1977   *Mode of Production and Social Formation: An Auto-Critique of Pre-Capitalist Modes of Production.* New York: Macmillan.

Hirschman, Albert
1961   *Latin American Issues: Essays and Comments.* New York: Twentieth Century Fund.

Hodges, Donald C.
1974   *The Latin American Revolution: Politics and Strategy from Apro-Marxism to Guevarism.* New York: William Morrow.

Hopkins, Terence K.
1977   "Notes on Class Analysis and the World-System." *Review* 1 (Summer), 67–72.

Hopkins, Terence K., and Immanuel Wallerstein
1977   "Patterns of Development of the Modern World-System." *Review* 1 (Fall), 111–145.

Horowitz, Irving Louis; Josué de Castro; and John Gerassi, eds.
1969   *Radicalism in Latin America: A Documentary Report on Left and Nationalist Movements.* New York: Random House.

Howe, Gary Niguel
1981   "Dependency Theory, Imperialism, and the Production of Surplus Value on a World Scale." *Latin American Perspectives* 8 (Summer and Fall), 82–102.

Hunt, Verl F.
1978   "The Rise of Feudalism in Eastern Europe: A Critical Appraisal of the Wallerstein 'World-System' Thesis." *Science and Society* 42 (Spring), 43–61.

Huntington, Samuel P.
1968   *Political Order in Changing Societies.* New Haven: Yale University Press.

Hymer, Stephen
1972   "The Internationalization of Capital." *Journal of Economic Issues* 6:1, 91–110.

Jalée, Pierre
1968   *The Pillage of the Third World.* Translated by Mary Klopper. New York: Monthly Review Press.

Johnson, Carlos
1981   "Dependency Theory and Processes of Capitalism and Socialism." *Latin American Perspectives* 8 (Summer and Fall), 55–81.

Johnson, Dale L.
1981   "Economism and Determinism in Dependency Theory." *Latin American Perspectives* 8 (Summer and Fall), 108–117.

Kahl, Joseph A.
1976   *Modernization, Exploitation, and Dependency in Latin America: Germani, González Casanova, and Cardoso.* New Brunswick, N.J.: Transaction Books.

Kay, Geoffrey
1975   *Development and Underdevelopment: A Marxist Analysis.* London: Macmillan.

Laclau, Ernesto
1971   "Feudalism and Capitalism in Latin America." *New Left Review* 67 (May-June), 19–38.

Lall, Sanjaya
1975   "Is 'Dependence' a Useful Concept in Analysing Underdevelopment?" *World Development* 3:11–12, 799–810.

Lane, David
1974   "Leninism as an Ideology of Soviet Development." Pp. 23–37 in Emmanuel De Kadt and Gavin Williams, eds., *Sociology and Development.* London: Tavistock Publications.

Leaver, Richard
1977   "The Debate on Underdevelopment: 'On Situation Gunder Frank.'"
        Journal of Contemporary Asia 7:1, 108–115.

Lenin, V. I.
1932   *State and Revolution.* New York: International Publishers.
1956   *The Development of Capitalism in Russia: The Process of the
        Formation of a Home Market for Large-Scale Industry.* Moscow:
        Foreign Languages Publishing House.
1967   *Selected Works.* 3 vols. Moscow: Progress Books.

Leys, Colin
1977   "Underdevelopment and Dependency: Critical Notes." *Journal of
        Contemporary Asia* 7:1, 92–107.

Lipset, Seymour Martin
1959   "Some Social Requisites of Democracy: Economic Development
        and Political Legitimacy." *American Political Science Review* 53
        (March), 69–105.

Love, Joseph L.
1980   "Raúl Prebisch and the Origins of the Doctrine of Unequal
        Exchange." *Latin American Research Review* 15:3, 45–72.

Lowy, Michael
1981   *The Politics of Combined and Uneven Development: The Theory
        of Permanent Revolution.* London: Verso.

Lustig, Nora
1980   "Underconsumption in Latin American Economic Thought: Some
        Considerations." *Review of Radical Political Economics* 12 (Spring),
        35–43.

Mandel, Ernest
1968   *Marxist Economic Theory.* 2 vols. New York: Monthly Review
        Press.
1970a   *Europe Versus America? Contradictions of Imperialism.* London:
        Monthly Review Press.
1970b   "The Laws of Uneven Development." *New Left Review* 59 (January-
        February), 19–38.
1972   *Decline of the Dollar: A Marxist View of the Monetary Crisis.*
        New York: Monad Press.
1974   *Du fascisme.* Paris: F. Maspero.
1975   *Late Capitalism.* London: NLB. Rev. ed., Verso, 1978.
1977   *From Class Society to Communism: An Introduction to Marxism.*
        London: Ink Links.
1978a   *Critique de l'eurocommunisme.* Paris: F. Maspero.
1978b   *De la Commune a Mai '68: histoire du mouvement ouvrier
        international.* Paris: Editions La Breche.

1978c   *From Stalinism to Eurocommunism: The Bitter Fruits of 'Socialism in One Country.'* London: NLB.

1978d   *The Second Slump: A Marxist Analysis of the Recession in the Seventies.* London: NLB.

1979   *Trotsky: A Study in the Dynamic of His Thought.* London: NLB.

Mandel, Ernest, ed.

1968   *Fifty Years of World Revolution, 1917–1967.* New York: Merit Publishers.

Marable, Manning

1983   *How Capitalism Underdeveloped Black America: Problems in Race, Political Economy, and Society.* Boston: South End Press.

Marcussen, Henrik Secher, and Jens Erik Torp

1982   *Internationalization of Capital—Prospects for the Third World: A Re-Examination of Dependency Theory.* London: Zed Press.

Marini, Ruy Mauro

1969   *Subdesarrollo y revolución.* Mexico City: Siglo Veintiuno Editores.

1973a   "Dependencia y subimperialismo en América Latina." *Cultura en México,* Supplement to *Siempre* 1030 (March 21), v–viii. Interview with Luis Angeles.

1973b   *Dialéctica de la dependencia.* Mexico City: Ediciones Era.

1976   *El reformismo y la contrarevolución: estudios sobre Chile.* Mexico City: Ediciones Era.

1978a   "Las razones del neodesarrollismo (respuesta a F. H. Cardoso y J. Serra)." *Revista Mexicana de Sociología* 40, 57–106.

1978b   "World Capitalist Accumulation and Sub-imperialism." *Two Thirds* 1 (Fall), 29–39.

Marini, Ruy Mauro, et al.

1973   *Tres ensayos sobre América Latina.* Barcelona: Editorial Anagrama.

Marx, Karl

1943   *Articles on India.* Bombay: People's Publishing House.

1967   *Capital: A Critique of Political Economy.* 3 vols. New York: International Publishers.

1974   *The First International and After.* Edited with an Introduction by David Fernbach. New York: Vintage Books.

1977–
1981   *Capital: A Critique of Political Economy.* 3 vols. New York: Vintage Books.

Marx, Karl, and Friedrich Engels

1958   "The Manifesto of the Communist Party." Pp. 33–65 in Vol. 1, *Selected Works in Two Volumes.* Moscow: Foreign Language Publishing House.

1972   *Ireland and the Irish Question.* Foreword by C. Desmond Greaves. Edited by R. Dixon. New York: International Publishers.

1973   *The German Ideology, Part One.* Edited with an Introduction by C. J. Arthur. New York: International Publishers.

1979   *Collected Works.* Vol. 12. New York: International Publishers.

Miliband, Ralph
1969   *The State in Capitalist Society: An Analysis of the Western System of Power.* New York: Basic Books.

Mohri, Kenzo
1979   "Marx and 'Underdevelopment.' " *Monthly Review* 30 (April), 32–42.

Montoya, Rodrigo
1982   "Class Relations in the Andean Countryside." *Latin American Perspectives* 9 (Summer), 62–78.

Moore, Joan W.
1970   "Colonialism: The Case of the Mexican Americans." *Social Problems* 17 (Spring), 463–472.

Munck, Ronaldo
1981   "Imperialism and Dependency: Recent Debates and Old Dead-ends." *Latin American Perspectives* 8 (Summer and Fall), 162–179.

Muni, S. D.
1979   "The Third World: Concept and Controversy." *Third World Quarterly* 1 (July), 119–128.

Myer, John
1975   "A Crown of Thorns: Cardoso and Counter-Revolution." *Latin American Perspectives* 2 (Spring), 47–48.

Nkrumah, Kwame
1968   "The Myth of the Third World." *Labour Monthly* 1 (October), 462–465.

Novack, George
1966   *Uneven and Combined Development in History.* New York: Merit Publishers.

1970   "The Permanent Revolution in Latin America." *Intercontinental Press* 8 (November 16), 978–983.

Nuti, D. M.
1969   "Review of Pierre Jalée, *The Pillage of the Third World.*" *Science and Society* 33 (Winter), 107–109.

O'Brien, Phillip
    1973   "Dependency: The New Nationalism?" *Latin American Review of Books* 1 (Spring), 35–41.
    1975   "A Critique of Latin American Theories of Dependency." Pp. 7–27 in Ivar Oxaal, Tony Barnett, and David Booth, eds., *Beyond the Sociology of Development*. London: Routledge and Kegan Paul.

O'Neill, John
    1969   "Introduction: Marxism and the Sociological Imagination." Pp. xiii–xxviii in Paul A. Baran, *The Longer View: Essays Toward a Critique of Political Economy*. New York: Monthly Review Press.

Organski, A.F.K.
    1965   *The Stages of Political Development*. New York: Alfred A. Knopf.

Ougaard, Morten
    1982–   "Some Remarks Concerning Peripheral Capitalism and the Pe-
    1983   ripheral State." *Science and Society* 46 (Winter), 385–404.

Packingham, Robert A.
    1982   "'Plus ça change . . . ' The English Edition of Cardoso and Faletto's *Dependencia y desarrollo en América Latina.*" *Latin American Research Review* 17:1, 131–151.

Palloix, Christian
    1975   *L'Internalisation du capital*. Paris: François Maspero. Spanish edition, *La internacionalización del capital*. Madrid: H. Blume Ediciones, 1978.
    1977   "The Self-Expansion of Capital on a World Scale." *Review of Radical Political Economy* 9 (Summer), 1–28. Translation of Chapter 2 and Appendix 1 from his book (1975).

Palma, Gabriel
    1978   "Dependency: A Formal Theory of Underdevelopment or a Methodology for the Analysis of Concrete Situations of Underdevelopment?" *World Development* 6:881–924.

Perroux, François
    1962   *L'économie des jeunes nations, industrialisation et groupements des nations*. Paris: n.p.
    1968   "Multinational Investment and the Analysis of Development and Integration Poles." Pp. 95–125 in Perroux, *Multinational Investment in the Economic Development and Integration of Latin America*. Bogotá: Inter-American Development Bank.

Petras, James
    1967   "The Roots of Underdevelopment." *Monthly Review* 9 (February), 49–55.
    1981   "Dependency and World System Theory: A Critique and New Directions." *Latin American Perspectives* 7 (Summer and Fall), 148–155.

Poulantzas, Nicos
1973   *Political Power and Social Classes.* London: New Left Books and Sheed and Ward.

Prado Júnior, Caio
1955   "Nacionalismo brasileiro e capitais estrangeiros." *Revista Brasiliense* 2 (November-December), 80–93.
1959   "Nacionalismo e desenvolvimento." *Revista Brasiliense* 24 (July-August), 9–15.
1962   *O mundo socialista.* 2d ed. São Paulo: Editôra Brasiliense.
1963   *Formaçáo do Brasil contemporaneo: colôn.a.* 7th ed. São Paulo: Editôra Brasiliense.
1966   *A revoluçáo brasileira.* São Paulo: Editôra Brasiliense.
1967   *The Colonial Background of Modern Brazil.* Translated by Suzette Macedo. Berkeley: University of California Press.
1969   "Contribuiçáo para añalise da questáo agrária no Brasil." Pp. 9–22 in Caio Prado Júnior et al., *A agricultura subdesenvolvida.* Petrópolis, Brazil: Editora Vozes Limitada.

Prebisch, Raúl
1978   "Notas sobre el desarrollo del capitalismo periférico." *Estudios Internacionales* 11 (July-September), 3–25.
1980   "The Dynamics of Peripheral Capitalism." Pp. 21–27 in Louis Lefeber and Liisa L. North, eds., *Democracy and Development in Latin America.* No. 1. Toronto: Studies on the Political Economy, Society and Culture of Latin America and the Caribbean.

Pye, Lucian W.
1966   *Aspects of Political Development.* Boston: Little, Brown and Company.

Quijano, Aníbal
1971   *Nationalism and Capitalism in Peru: A Study in Neo-Imperialism.* New York: Monthly Review Press.
1972   *Dependencia, urbanización y cambio social en Latinoamérica.* Lima: Mosca Azul Editores.
1974   "Imperialism and International Relations in Latin America." Pp. 67–91 in Julio Cotler and Richard Fagan, eds., *Latin America and the Changing Political Realities.* Stanford: Stanford University Press.
1975   *Imagen y tareas del sociólogo en la sociedad peruana.* Lima: Pontificia Universidad Católica del Perú.
1976a   *Clase obrera en América Latina.* San José, Costa Rica: Editorial Universitaria Centroamericana.
1976b   *Crise imperialista e classe operária na América Latina.* Coimbra, Portugal: Centelho.
1977   *Imperialismo y "marginalidad" en América Latina.* Lima: Mosca Azul Editores.

1979 *Problema agrario y movimientos campesinos.* Lima: Mosca Azul Editores.

1980 "1980: las condiciones del enfrentamiento." *Sociedad y Política* 3 (February), 6–15.

Rey, Pierre-Philippe
1973 *Les alliances de classes.* Paris: Maspero.

Rodney, Walter
1967 *West Africa and the Atlantic Slave Trade.* Nairobi: Historical Association of Tanzania, East African Publishing House.

1970 *A History of the Upper Guinea Coast, 1545–1800.* Oxford: Clarendon Press.

1972 *How Europe Underdeveloped Africa.* London: Bogle-L'Ouverture Publications; Dar es Salaam: Tanzania Publishing House.

1975 *The Groundings with My Brothers.* Introduction by Richard Small. London: Bogle-L'Ouverture Publications.

1981a *A History of the Guyanese Working People, 1881–1905.* Baltimore: Johns Hopkins University Press.

1981b "People's Power, No Dictator." *Latin American Perspectives* 8 (Winter), 64–78.

Rodriguez O., Gustavo
1980 "Original Accumulation, Capitalism, and Precapitalistic Agriculture in Bolivia." *Latin American Perspectives* 7 (Fall), 50–66.

Rojas, Antonio
1980 "Land and Labor in the Articulation of the Peasant Economy with the Hacienda." *Latin American Perspectives* 7 (Fall), 67–82.

Rose, Arnold M.
1967 *The Power Structure: Political Process in American Society.* London: Oxford University Press.

Rostow, Walt W.
1960 *The Stages of Economic Growth: A Non-Communist Manifesto.* Cambridge: Cambridge University Press.

Roxborough, Ian
1979 *Theories of Underdevelopment.* Atlantic Highlands, N.J.: Humanities Press.

Samuelson, Paul
1976 "Illogic of Neo-Marxian Doctrine of Unequal Exchange." Pp. 96–107 in David A. Belsley et al., eds., *Inflation, Trade, and Taxes.* Columbus: Ohio State University Press.

Sau, Ranjit
1975 "Capitalism, Imperialism, and Underdevelopment." *Economic and Political Weekly* nos. 33–35:1263–1276.

Serra, José, and Fernando Henrique Cardoso
1978   "Las desventuras de la dialéctica de la dependencia." *Revista Mexicana de Sociología* 40:9–95.

Sica, Alan
1978   "Review Essay: Dependency in the World Economy." *American Journal of Sociology* 84 (November), 728–739.

Sindico, Domenico E.
1977   "New Left Theories on the Mode of Production." *Studies in Marxism* 1:95–102.
1980   "Modernization in Nineteenth-Century Sugar Haciendas: The Case of Morelos (from Formal to Real Subsumption of Labor to Capital)." *Latin American Perspectives* 7 (Fall), 83–99.

Skinner, Quentin
1979   "Taking Off." *New York Review of Books* 26 (March 22), 15.

Sombart, Werner
1928   *Der moderne Kapitalismus.* Vol. 3, *Das Wirtschaftsleben im Zeitalter des Hochkapitalismus.* Munich: n.p.

Stone, John
1979   "Introduction: Internal Colonialism in Comparative Perspective." *Ethnic and Racial Studies* 2 (April), 254–259.

Sunkel, Osvaldo
1970   "Transitional Capitalism and National Disintegration in Latin America." Paper presented to a student conference sponsored by the Latin American Center, University of California, Los Angeles, at Lake Arrowhead, California.
1972   "Big Business and 'Dependencia.'" *Foreign Affairs* 50 (April), 517–531.
1977   "El desarrollo de la teoria del desarrollo." *Estudios Latinoamericanos* 40 (December), 33–46.

Sunkel, Osvaldo, with Pedro Paz
1970   *El subdesarrollo latinoamericano y la teoria del desarrollo.* Madrid: Siglo Veintiuno de España Editores.

Sweezy, Paul M.
1965   "Paul Alexander Baran: A Personal Memoir." *Monthly Review* 16 (March), 28–62.

Sweezy, Paul M., and Charles Bettelheim
1971   *On the Transition to Socialism.* New York: Monthly Review Press.

Sweezy, Paul M., and Leo Huberman, eds.
1965   *Paul Baran (1910–1965): A Collective Portrait.* New York: Monthly Review Press.

Taylor, John G.
1979   *From Modernization to Modes of Production: A Critique of the Sociologies of Development and Underdevelopment.* New York: Macmillan.

Thomas, Clive Y.
1978   "'The Non-Capitalist Path' as Theory and Practice of Decolonization and Socialist Transformation." *Latin American Perspectives* 5 (Spring), 10–28.

Trotsky, Leon
1929   *The Draft Program of the Communist International: A Criticism of Fundamentals.* New York: Militant.
1959   *The Russian Revolution.* Garden City, N.Y.: Doubleday, Anchor.
1962   *The Permanent Revolution.* New York: Pioneer Publishers.
1964   "The Theory of Permanent Revolution." Pp. 62–65 in Isaac Deutscher, ed., *The Age of Permanent Revolution: A Trotsky Anthology.* New York: Dell Publishing.

Vitale, Luis
1963   *Esencia y apariencia de la Democracia Cristiana.* Santiago, Chile: Arancibia Hmnos.
1967   *Interpretación marxista de la historia de Chile.* Vol. 1, *Las culturas primitivas, de conquista española.* Santiago, Chile: Prensa Latinoamericana.
1968   "Latin America: Feudal or Capitalist?" Pp. 32–43 in James Petras and Maurice Zeitlin, eds., *Latin America: Reform or Revolution?* Greenwich, Conn.: Fawcett Publications.
1971a   "España antes y después de la conquista de América." Pp. 1–25 in Luis Vitale et al., *Feudalismo, capitalismo, subdesarrollo.* Ibagué, Colombia: Universidad de Tolima.
1971b   *Interpretación marxista de la historia de Chile.* Vol. 3, *La independencia política, la rebelión de las provincias y la burguesía comercial y terrateniente.* Santiago, Chile: Prensa Latinoamericana.

Wallerstein, Immanuel
1961   *Africa, the Politics of Independence: An Interpretation of Modern African History.* New York: Vintage Books.
1966   *Social Change: The Colonial Situation.* New York: John Wiley and Sons.
1967   *Africa: The Politics of Unity, an Analysis of a Contemporary Social Movement.* New York: Random House.
1972   "Three Paths of National Development in Sixteenth-Century Europe." *Studies in Comparative International Development* 7 (Summer), 95–102.
1974a   *The Modern World-System.* Vol. 1, *Capitalist Agriculture and the Origins of the European World-Economy in the Sixteenth Century.* New York: Academic Press.

1974b   "The Rise and Future Demise of the World Capitalist System: Concepts for Comparative Analysis." *Comparative Studies in Society and History* 16 (September), 387–415.

1975   "Class-Formation in the Capitalist World-Economy." *Politics and Society* 5:3, 367–375.

1976   "From Feudalism to Capitalism: Transition or Transitions?" *Social Forces* 55 (December), 273–283.

1979   *The Capitalist World Economy: Essays.* New York: Cambridge University Press.

1980   *The Modern World-System.* Vol. 2, *Mercantilism and Consolidation of the European World-Economy, 1600–1750.* New York: Academic Press.

Wallerstein, Immanuel, and Peter C.W. Gutkind, eds.
1976   *The Political Economy of Africa.* Beverly Hills, Calif.: Sage Publications.

Warren, Bill
1973   "Imperialism and Capitalist Industrialization." *New Left Review* 81 (September-October), 3–44.

1980   *Imperialism: Pioneer of Capitalism.* Edited by John Sender. London: NLB.

Weber, Max
1958   *From Max Weber: Essays in Sociology.* Translated and edited with an Introduction by H. H. Gerth and C. Wright Mills. New York: Oxford University Press.

Weeks, John
1981   "The Differences Between Materialist Theory and Dependency Theory and Why They Matter." *Latin American Perspectives* 8 (Summer and Fall), 118–123.

Weffort, Francisco C.
1971   "Notas sôbre a 'teoria de dependência': teoria de classe ou ideologia nacional?" Pp. 3–24 in Fernando Henrique Cardoso et al. *Sôbre teoria e método em sociologia.* São Paulo: Edições CEBRAP.

Wolf-Phillips, Leslie
1979   "Why Third World?" *Third World Quarterly* 1 (January), 105–109. Reprinted in Leslie Wolf-Phillips et al. (1980).

Wolf-Phillips, Leslie, et al.
1980   *Why Third World?* Monograph no. 7. London: Third World Foundation.

Worsley, Peter
    1980   "One World or Three? A Critique of the World-System Theory of
             Immanuel Wallerstein." Pp. 298–338 in Ralph Miliband and John
             Saville, eds., *The Socialist Register 1980*. London: Merlin Press.

Wright, Erik Olin
    1980   "Varieties of Marxist Conception of Class Structure." *Politics and
             Society* 9:3, 323–370.

Glossary of Terms

Throughout this book I have attempted to explain and clarify the meaning of terms as they evolved in the conceptualization and theory of each thinker. Where there is a difference in meaning in the use of a term in the thought of more than one writer, I discuss the implications and variance in the use of such terminology. However, I generally do not redefine and explain terms after they first appear in the text. Thus, the list of terms below may help the reader.

Absolute surplus value. Value derived from the lengthening of the working day without increasing the daily wage (cf. *Relative surplus value*).

Accumulation. The process whereby the capitalist sells his commodities and converts the money from the sale into capital.

Associated dependent capitalism. Situation in the periphery in which the domestic bourgeoisie ties itself to capitalism, associates with international capital, and stimulates capitalist accumulation. Accumulation and expansion of local capital thus depend on the dynamic of international capitalism (cf. *Dependency*).

Backwardness. Characterization used by Baran and others to describe conditions of exploitation and underdevelopment in some countries.

Bourgeois democratic revolution. The stage of parliamentary democracy or social democracy in which proletarian forces support bourgeois rule and reformist action en route to socialism.

Bourgeoisie. The capitalist class, the class of owners of the means of production, and the employers of wage labor under capitalism.

Capitalism. Characterized by the formation of a bourgeois class that owns and controls the means of production and a class of producers that owns only its labor and must sell its labor power to the owners of the means of production in order to survive.

Circulation of capital. Capital, for example, commodity capital within the sphere of circulation, that is on the market. Usually refers to trade market and circulation of capital. According to Marx, "Commercial capital, then, is nothing but the transformed form of a portion of this circulation capital which is always to be found on the market, in the course of its metamorphosis, and perpetually confined to the circulation sphere" (Marx 1981, 3:380).

Class. Group or groups characterized by similar socioeconomic criteria such as income and status. Marx believed that under capitalism, society would eventually polarize into two classes, the bourgeoisie and the proletariat. Max Weber described class in a market situation and emphasized status groups within a class. These writers and others refer to many classes. A ruling class, for example, is an economic class that rules politically; it tends to be a class of varied interests that become cohesive. Other classes may include the monopolistic, agrarian, mining, industrial, and commercial bourgeoisies; the petty bourgeoisie; the new middle class or new petty bourgeoisie; proletariat; peasants; and lumpen proletariat (see Chapter 1 for definitions of these terms).

Colonial dependency. Situation in which the land, mines, and labor of a colony are tied to the mother country through trade monopolies.

Communism. A type of society characterized by the elimination of a commodity and money economy; the disappearance of inequality, classes, and the state; the overcoming of alienation in work; and the creative use of work and leisure.

Competitive capitalism. Capitalism with "free" competition, usually under small-scale enterprise, in contrast to the tendency to concentrate capital through cartels, trusts, and holding companies under monopoly capitalism.

Dependency. Situation in which accumulation and expansion of capital are undynamic, the result being dependency on the dominant countries that can expand and be self-sustaining (cf. *Associated dependent capitalism, Colonial dependency, Financial-Industrial dependency, New dependency*).

Development of underdevelopment. The thesis of André Gunder Frank and others that capitalism generates economic growth in the metropolis center through the appropriation of the economic surplus of the satellites, thereby contributing to stagnancy and underdevelopment in the periphery.

Diffusionist development. The view that political and economic democracy, nationalist development, and modernization will result from the diffusion of capital and technology from advanced to backward nations.

Dual society. A society considered to have two separate economies, one feudalistic in the countryside and the other capitalistic in the cities.

Economic surplus. As defined by Baran, the difference between a society's output and its consumption.

Enclave economy. An economy in which foreign capital has penetrated into the local productive processes in the form of wages and taxes to ensure exports of raw materials or goods.

Finance capital. Bank capital that penetrates and dominates industry.

Financial-industrial dependency. A situation in which big bank and industrial capital dominated and expanded outside the hegemonic centers during the period from the end of the nineteenth century to the Second World War.

Forces of production. Productive capacity, including plants and machinery, technology, and labor skills (cf. *Means of production, Mode of production*).

Imperialism. As defined by Lenin, monopoly capitalism, the highest stage of capitalism, usually associated with the appearance of cartels, trusts, and holding companies and the growth of industrial monopolies; alternatively, the military and political expansion of aggressive nations beyond their borders (cf. *Monopoly capitalism*).

Import substitution. Protection of domestic industry through the implementation of tariffs and the encouraging of local industry to meet demands for consumer goods.

Infrastructure. The economic structures in which the relations of production and material foundations are found and upon which, according to Marx, the legal and political superstructures arise; as used by the ECLA economists, the roads, power, and other resources that permit industrialization.

Internal colonialism. A relationship similar to the colonial relationship between nations but involving dominant and marginal groups within a single society (for example, according to González Casanova, the monopoly of the ruling metropolis in Mexico over the marginal Indian communities).

Labor power. Capacity of work, including skills, owned by the class of producers who, under capitalism, must sell it to the owners of the means of production in order to survive.

Late capitalism. As defined by Mandel, the capitalism of the post–Second World War period, characterized by the rise of the multinational firm.

Marginality. As used by Quijano and González Casanova, the situation of peoples (usually Indians) who do not participate politically and economically in the national society.

Means of production. The tools, land, buildings, machinery, and raw materials with which workers produce goods for themselves and the society (see *Mode of production, Forces of production*).

Merchant capital. An elementary form of capitalism associated with the introduction of money and the appearance of the merchant in international commerce.

Mode of production. The mix of productive forces and relations of production in a society at a given time in history. Modes may include primitive communism, feudalism, capitalism, and communism (cf. *Forces of production, Means of production*).

Monopoly capitalism. A form of capitalism characterized by the rise of cartels, trusts, and holding companies and the growth of industrial monopolies.

National bourgeoisie. The domestic class of "progressive" capitalists within a nation whose interests presumably are not tied to international capital but are associated with the development of national resources and industrialization.

Necessary production. Production for the subsistence of workers—their food, shelter, and so on (cf. *Surplus production*).

New dependency. Dependency characterized by capital investment of multinational corporations in industries oriented to the internal market of underdeveloped countries in the period after the Second World War (cf. *Dependency*).

Peripheral capitalism. As defined by Prebisch and others, an imitative capitalism in the backward countries in which capitalism is unable to reproduce itself and capital accumulation is incompatible with the consumer society (cf. *Capitalism*).

Permanent revolution. As advocated by Leon Trotsky, the revolution that eventually occurs everywhere as a means of overcoming class rule and advancing rapidly toward socialism.

Petty-commodity production. The production by professional artisans of commodities that they exchange freely for products they need.

Poles of development. As defined by François Perroux, the establishment of industrial centers in outlying regions and rural areas through the diffusion of capital and technology.

Primitive accumulation. The process whereby the possession of the means of production is taken from the workers or producers in the early stages of capitalism, thus breaking down the precapitalist social formation.

Proletariat. A class of workers who only own their labor and must sell this to the owners of the means of production in order to survive.

Relations of production. The division of labor that puts productive forces in motion. (cf. *Means of production*).

Relative surplus value. Value derived from production of a given amount of material goods in fewer hours through efficiency, technology, or the like (cf. *Absolute surplus value*).

Reproduction of capital. Process in which a capitalist society, in order to continue producing, must reproduce itself by replacing equipment, raw materials, and other essentials used in production. In production, workers consume the means of production or raw materials that go into their product; with their wages, they also consume in order to obtain food and shelter; and the capitalist consumes labor power or pays for the labor that is used in the production process.

Socialism. Collective and public rather than individual and private ownership of the means of production and appropriation of the surplus product (cf. *Transition to socialism*).

State. Originally evolved when the functions of people in primitive communal societies were assumed by separate groups of people such as armies, judges, and hereditary rulers. Hegel, Marx, and Engels saw the state as emerging from the civil society as a separate entity of apparatuses and activities. An instrumentalist approach to the study of the state emphasizes that the state is only an instrument manipulated by the ruling classes, whereas the structuralist approach stresses that the bourgeois ruling class is unable to dominate the state and the state unifies and organizes the interests of that class through structures or apparatuses such as the army, police, and judiciary.

Structuralism. The approach of political economists to analyzing the world in terms of centers and peripheries, metropoles and satellites; alternatively, in some Marxist writings, the repressive, political, and ideological apparatuses of the capitalist state.

Subimperialism. As defined by Marini, a situation in which the prospects for industrialization in a dependent capitalist economy are not great, and therefore the economy attempts to expand by pushing beyond its national borders and dominate the economies of weaker neighbors.

Superstructure. The legal, political, religious, philosophical, or ideological forms that, according to Marx, arise out of the infrastructure or economic base of society (cf. *Infrastructure*).

Surplus production. The production of workers beyond their requirements for subsistence (cf. *Necessary production*).

Third World. As defined in this volume, a condition of exploitation and oppression, a lack of technology and development, underdevelopment brought about through colonialism and imperialism, and dependency on the dominant capitalist world system.

Transition to socialism. Period in which a workers' state replaces the capitalist state, the means of production come under collective rather than private ownership, and proletarian democracy replaces bourgeois democracy, though remnants of capitalism such as a money economy may persist.

Underconsumption. Traditionally, a condition in which domestic consumption is unable to absorb the products of industrialized nations, thus necessitating imperialism in the search for markets in the exploited colonies and outlying areas; more recently, an explanation for underdevelopment in backward countries in which a bourgeoisie's consumption is limited.

Index

DATE DUE

APR 9 1987			
SEP 2 4 1987			
DEC 7 1990			